INSIDE OUT AND UPSIDE DOWN LEADERSHIP

TORN CURTAIN PUBLISHING
Auckland, New Zealand
www.torncurtainpublishing.com

ISBN Softcover 978-1-991299-10-9
ISBN EPub 978-1-991299-11-6

The material in chapters two and three is largely based on *A History of the Apostolic Church Movement in NZ* compiled by the late Mr Rex Meehan. This unpublished pamphlet draws significantly from a research project undertaken by Ps. Sheridyn Rodgers in 1995.

Front cover design icons from the Noun Project. Used with Permission.
Typeset in Minion Pro, Myriad Pro, Minion Std.

Co-authored by Jeffrey McKee and edited by Anya McKee.

Cataloguing in Publishing Data
Title: Inside Out and Upside Down Leadership: Lessons and experiences from sixteen years of reforming and liberating an apostolic movement
Author: Bruce Monk
Themes: Christian Living / Leadership & Mentoring; Christian Church / History; Christian Theology / Ecclesiology
Subjects: Contemporary Church Leadership, Apostolic Church History, ACTS Churches NZ, Kingdom Culture, Fivefold Leadership, Institutional Reform, Charitable Trusts in NZ, Distributed Leadership Models, Ecclesiastical Structures, Christian Organisational Models, Christian Leadership and Formation, Global Christian Movements.

A copy of this title is held at the National Library of New Zealand.

INSIDE OUT AND UPSIDE DOWN LEADERSHIP

Lessons and experiences from sixteen years of reforming and liberating an apostolic movement

BRUCE MONK

WITH JEFFREY MCKEE

"Now these are the gifts Christ gave to the church: the apostles, the prophets, the evangelists, and the pastors and teachers. Their responsibility is to equip God's people to do his work and build up the church, the body of Christ."

— Ephesians 4:11-12 (NLT)

Contents

In the early years of the twentieth century, a move of God in the mining villages of Wales set in motion a wave of Pentecostal expansion that circled the globe. Known as the Welsh Revival, it had far-reaching consequences that included New Zealand in its embrace. Out of this move was birthed the Apostolic Church in Britain, and in the late 1920s, the first Apostolic Church in New Zealand was established in Wellington.

Over the past century, through many leadership changes, the Apostolic Church in New Zealand has grown to become a movement of churches committed to equipping and releasing another generation of men and women into their God-given callings.

Today, the ACTS Church Movement is comprised of a network of 60+ churches across New Zealand, including Equippers Churches and other networks, all equally moving forward together and sharing the same values around the cornerstone scripture of Ephesians 4:11-12.

This is our story.

Introduction

In 2001, just five months after my wife Helen and I had moved to London to assume the leadership of a young church, I returned home to New Zealand to attend the annual council meeting of our church movement.

I knew this would be no ordinary meeting. Our national leader at the time had indicated that he would not be standing for re-election, and as a council, our job was to appoint his successor.

For many years I had carried a vision for the Apostolic Church movement in New Zealand. Now I was caught in a tension. On one hand, Helen and I strongly believed the Holy Spirit had inspired our move to the United Kingdom only five months earlier. On the other hand, the way seemed open to bring the change I knew was necessary—to reconnect with our roots in the Welsh Revival and create an environment where subsequent generations could thrive. This vacancy presented the opportunity to lead and reform the movement.

At that council meeting, I was nominated along with one other person, and after due process, I was appointed to the role of national leader, which I held for the next sixteen years. This book is my reflection on the challenges of that position, and what we achieved as we partnered with the Lord, along with the overarching principles I employed in that role. In these pages, you will gain insight into the significant changes that took place during the period when I led the Apostolic Movement in New Zealand. For some, it may also serve as a how-to manual. This book provides threads of perspective. It is a chance to look over my shoulder as I led the National Leadership Team, and with them faced some of the most significant challenges of my life.

Together we outworked a very precious vision and implemented structure and governance that stripped away the hindrances that were stifling leadership within our movement at the time. I hope this book will provide a helpful perspective on revival culture, and that it will feed your faith and encourage you to also step up with confidence when called to lead.

One of the reasons this book is in your hands is that I have been privileged to be both called to outwork a vision *and* appointed to a role where I was empowered to do so. I praise God for that. When my time to lead had concluded, I stepped down knowing that the vision had been fulfilled.

As a movement, we know that revival is in our heritage, but over the years, in our attempt to steward the fruits of revival, we had become more and more institutionalised, setting up structures that interrupted 'apostolic immediacy' and stifled God's appointed agents of revival, the apostles among us. Even though in name we valued our apostles, as a movement, we were frustrating them.

Apostolic immediacy has been key in every move of God, and the Welsh Revival, which we sprung from, is no exception. When God has a plan, His apostles intuitively catch hold of His vision. They quickly perceive what He wants to do and how He wants to get it done. Instinctively, they spring into action and rally others to join in and help. It is the immediacy of their response that quickly builds a foundation for others, creating the momentum necessary for revival to reach a tipping point and truly break out.

In institutionalising revival, we had constrained our apostles by centrally controlling what was intended to be distributed and responsive, unstoppable and organic. We had boxed-in apostolic initiative—cutting ourselves off from what we truly desired to be defined by. Our vision was to restore the priority of apostolic immediacy and apostolic initiatives. This book allows you to climb aboard with us on the journey as we took deliberate action to unshackle the apostles among us—as we set up governance and structure for our movement in New Zealand—and so reclaimed our birthright.

To make this as useful a resource as possible to as many as possible, I begin in the first part by setting the scene. How did Helen and I come to be part of the movement and its leadership? How did Equippers (the church Helen and I founded) affect my appointment to the role of National leader? Why had the movement become constrained? How did I catch a vision for change? And finally, why was I still around when so many other apostles had grown frustrated and left?

The next two parts can be divided chronologically. Part two recounts the years after I was appointed the national leader of our movement. During this time, we focused on cultural change and laid the foundation for the structural reforms—recounted in part three—that restored and released apostolic immediacy among us.

Finally, in part four, I highlight the impact these changes have had on the movement since. In this section, you will find key insights and activations that I would like to gift to future generations of leaders who will need to vigilantly guard the lifeblood of revival, just as I have sought to do.

My desire is that you will discover the story of a movement that now releases and enables our people to be true to themselves, flourishing together and energetically pursuing the work they have been called to do.

— Bruce Monk

VISION AND CALLING

1

Firmly Planted

One Sunday morning soon after Helen and I were married, we decided to attend our local Anglican Church where a newly appointed minister was holding his first service. In his sermon that day, the minister spoke clearly about the way of salvation. I had first encountered Christ when I was twelve at a youth club called *Every Boy's Rally,* but I had never fully heard or understood the gospel. That day, something clicked. Helen and I responded positively to the minister's message, and for both of us, this marked the beginning of a brand-new life.

ENCOUNTERING THE HOLY SPIRIT

As part of the Anglican Church, we soon found ourselves embracing what is now known as the Charismatic Renewal Movement. This renewal was sweeping across the globe and impacting many churches like our own that were traditional but open to something fresh and new. One night soon after I responded to the message of salvation, I was at a house group where some friends gathered around and prayed for me to be baptised in the Holy Spirit. God answered that prayer, and I experienced an overwhelming flow of joy filling my heart.

The effects of that moment were lasting. I was a dairy farmer—and to my surprise, the very next morning when I reached to push the start button on the milking machine, I immediately started speaking in tongues. I'm sure the cows never forgot the new sound they heard that day! Later that year I was baptised in water, and that too was accompanied by a powerful encounter with the Holy Spirit.

SHAPED BY GOD'S WORD

As Helen and I progressed in our spiritual journey, the Holy Spirit began confronting us about areas in our lives that needed to change, and guiding us toward transformation, breakthrough, and freedom. Helen and I were like sponges, soaking up God's Word wherever we could. At that time, meetings were springing up everywhere around the region, and a constant flow of excellent national and international speakers was being welcomed at a Christian campsite only fifteen minutes from where we lived. We also had a growing group of charismatic Christians surrounding us at church. It was a powerful season in New Zealand—and in our lives. Through His people and His Word, God was giving us keys that would empower our lives well into the future. It was during this time that I learnt to pray and to regularly fast, and I built the Word of God into my life. Our church had never taught on the subject of tithing, but when Helen and I read Malachi 3:8-10 the Holy Spirit encouraged us to embrace this discipline, and to this day we still honour the Lord with our first fruits. These were disciplines that would stand me in good stead for the years ahead.

JOINING THE APOSTOLIC CHURCH

As the Holy Spirit graciously led us down a pathway of new beginnings, I began to experience His incredible power in my everyday life. The first sermon I ever preached was in our little Anglican Church, and a woman responded by giving her heart to Christ. Things were ramping up quickly for us, but over the next few years, our minister, who was at first enthusiastic about this move of God, started to push back against the Charismatic movement. That church had always been so life-giving for Helen and me, but it soon became very uncomfortable for us. Knowing it was time for us to leave, we looked around and found the only option in our small township was to join the local apostolic church. This church had no more than fifteen people and no local leader at the time—although John Douglas, a Pentecostal pastor from the nearby town of Levin, provided oversight and pastoral care for this rural congregation as well as his own. Eventually, after much prayer, we decided to move on from the Anglican community that had been so pivotal in our journey and to make our home in the apostolic church instead.

While the apostolic church boasted a greater freedom of worship than we had experienced under the liturgical tradition of the Anglican Church, it wasn't long before we discovered this assembly also had a liturgy of its own, though one not taken from a book. All the elders would sit along the front, and one would go to sleep every Sunday soon after the sermon started—the same man who stood up every week to give the congregation 'a word'! But on the positive side, the preaching and teaching were Bible-based and anointed.

We were growing, and the church was too. Before long, more than fifty people were regularly attending our local apostolic church. God was so evidently at work! Prayer groups were popping up, the Word of God was alive and changing lives, prophetic ministry was flowing, testimonies of healing and miracles became commonplace, and in the space of two years, twenty-two of my family members gave their hearts to Christ! There was a sense of revival, and it was spreading. Helen and I regularly rallied the young people from our region and took them to Wellington for Youth for Christ meetings, and then on to Palmerston North where large-scale renewal meetings were being held at the racecourse. We were right in the centre of what God was doing, and we couldn't have been happier.

THE CALL OF GOD

Despite the excitement of this season, the Holy Spirit was already stirring our hearts toward a larger vision. I remember receiving a strong prophetic word from one of my ex-schoolteachers, that I would be a 'sent one' and that the Holy Spirit would release me into the nations of the world. Gradually it began to dawn on me that God had called me as an 'apostle', and even though I had very limited knowledge of what that entailed, it was soon confirmed by the prophetic ministry of others. At one point, I received the same prophetic word from five different people in five different locations. Each time, the person directly quoted a scripture:

> *Trust in the Lord with all your heart, and lean not on your own understanding; In all your ways acknowledge Him, and He shall direct your paths.*
>
> — PROVERBS 3:5-6

At first, my response was, "That's just what someone says when they are not sure what to say." But when I was given the same verse a fifth time, there was no doubt in my mind that I was being given a prophetic word. This served and helped stir and direct the call of God on my life. In the years that followed, the Holy Spirit used this scripture as a strong anchor for me in times of uncertainty, especially when my understanding has defaulted to natural reasoning or got out of step with God's higher perspective. God has often shown me plans based on His understanding and view of things, and I could never have embraced them without an absolute trust in His ability to navigate on my behalf.

TE NIKAU BIBLE COLLEGE

When we realised the call of God on our lives was becoming even stronger, Helen and I decided that I would attend *Te Nikau Bible College* in Paraparaumu for a year. This college was associated with the Apostolic Church movement, and the principal was our pastor, John Douglas. It was early days for the college, and things were not fine-tuned or particularly well organised, but I found the teaching exceptional. I was one of four in my class, and we had enrolled in the first course they offered, so everything was 'up close and personal', and to this day, I sincerely value the foundation I received during that year.

One of the major reasons we chose to study at *Te Nikau* was that it was only a fifteen-minute drive from our home. This meant I could continue to oversee the running of our dairy farm and work alongside the full-time worker we had employed—but it became a challenging year for our family, with four preschool-age children at home, as well as my studies. Helen often says she had the best possible Bible college experience because of the increased pressure she had to shoulder in my absence during this time. Most of all, we were both determined to keep growing in our capacity.

A PIVOTAL INVITATION

When my year of Bible college came to an end, Helen and I contracted my brother-in-law as a share milker on our property and moved our family to Gisborne, where I was given the opportunity to work as an intern in a church of more than two hundred people. Over ninety percent of the congregation were Māori, the Indigenous people of New Zealand. This was a very rich experience, and it became a fruitful year. The pastor, Howard Arnold, was a beautiful man with a strong pastoral grace on his life. His approach wasn't as structured as I deemed necessary in outworking the vision he had, but we worked well together. His maturity balanced my youthful zeal, and my tendency toward structure was complemented by his love for people.

It was in the middle of our year in Gisborne that my dad suddenly died of a heart attack. This was life-changing for me. My father had sowed so much of himself into me and passed on so many practical insights. I had grown up on the family farm alongside him, but the calling on our lives was clear. Our farming days were now in the past.

As the year in Gisborne came to an end, Helen and I heard that the apostolic church in Whanganui had recently closed, and because we were still supported by our farm, we decided to make ourselves available to reopen the church without any cost to the movement. This was to be our first church plant and the beginning of a journey into church leadership. It was all a steep learning curve, and my library grew rapidly as I tried to glean all I could from others who had done this before. Gradually, I began to better understand the gifts God had given me and the operation of His grace upon my life. During our Whanganui years, we had to navigate some major areas of conflict with those who wanted to adjust the vision and culture we had defined for the church to suit their personal agendas. Looking back, I am very thankful for this foundational period of my life.

A few years later, around 1981, I was invited to join the Council of the Apostolic Church in New Zealand. I was unusually young for such an invitation, but Helen and I were progressive in our approach and experiencing a reasonable level of success, and thankfully, the council valued a voice that represented the emerging generation.

2

Rooted in Revival

The roots of the Apostolic Church Movement lie deep in the past, at a time when God was moving mightily in the country of Wales. The *Welsh Revival*, as it has become known, occurred between 1904 and 1905. This intense visitation from God resulted in people coming to Christ in droves. As a result, the cultural landscape of Wales was completely turned around. As Edwin Orr reported, "It revolutionised an entire nation; hundreds of thousands were saved; drunkards, thieves, gamblers were transformed; pubs went out of business and the courts were void of cases.[1]"

LOCKED OUT

The Welsh Revival became part of a global outpouring of the Holy Spirit. In 1907-08, after the initial revival had passed its peak, a 'second visitation' took place. The dramatic impact was felt in North America, South Africa, India, Europe and many other places as people began to experience a baptism in the Holy Spirit. This manifested—as it does today—with speaking in tongues, prophecy, healing, interpretation of tongues, and discerning of spirits. Around the world, many were uncomfortable with these raw demonstrations of the Spirit's power. Those who were baptised in the Holy Spirit were often treated with suspicion and turned away from

---

1   J. Edwin Orr, *Re-study of Revival and Revivalism*, School of World Mission, Pasadena, 1981.

the established churches, so they met where they could, in their homes or rented halls. It was the challenge posed by this second move of God that was pivotal to the formation of the Apostolic Movement.

These fledgling communities celebrated their newly discovered freedom within the Pentecostal experience, but unfortunately, excesses and extreme behaviour in some places brought ridicule and condemnation toward the entire group. Godly Pentecostal leaders became greatly concerned. Realising that some of the criticism was justified, some swung to the other extreme, forbidding any manifestation of the Holy Spirit.

A VOICE IN THE WILDERNESS

At this point, Daniel Powell Williams became an important character in the history of the Apostolic Church Movement's formation. Daniel was saved on Christmas Day 1904 at the age of twenty-two when the Welsh Revival was in its first year. A little later, while working deep underground in the coal mines of Wales, he heard God say, "You are to preach." Acting in obedience, Daniel began touring across the country, and over the next six years, ministered among almost eighty chapel congregations. He was not caught up in the second phase of the revival, but while away on holiday from his usual ministry, he received the baptism of the Holy Spirit. At the time, he was with some Pentecostal friends who had already felt the touch and power of the Holy Spirit. Sitting on a hillside above the sea with his friends, Daniel had an encounter with the Holy Spirit and began to speak in tongues. This experience impacted his life and ministry greatly. When he returned to his hometown of Penygroes, he started meeting with the Pentecostals.

Two years later, Daniel left mining to become a full-time minister. Along with other Pentecostal leaders, he believed that the phenomenon of the Spirit was truly from God. However, these leaders recognised that for His power to have its full effect there must be some degree of regulation and direction. They believed that the gifts and ministry of the Holy Spirit should operate in a context of divine order.

HOLDING ONTO THE FUNDAMENTALS

Daniel and his brother, W. Jones Williams, began to seek God for a way forward. At the time, they couldn't imagine a structure that could provide a fitting context for the operation of the very dynamic and often dramatic ministry of the Holy Spirit. As they prayed, God gave them a revelation of 'five-fold leadership' as a reflection of divine government. They saw Christ's ascension gifts (see Ephesians 4:11) as a God-given pattern, with each role demonstrating an aspect of the 'headship' of Jesus Christ to the community. This prophetic revelation was both *predictive* and *directive*— they understood what God was planning to do, as well as how they were to participate in His plans.

Later that year, Daniel and his brother formed a connection with a group called the *Apostolic Faith Churches* of Bournemouth, England. Soon, all the Welsh churches associated with Daniel joined the same group. Unfortunately, five years later, Daniel and nineteen of the Welsh congregations withdrew from them because of disagreements regarding leadership style, property ownership, and approaches to financial management[2]. Some sources also indicate that prophetic direction prompted this move.

THE NATURE OF FIVE-FOLD LEADERSHIP

Five-fold church leadership can operate at different levels, but by its very nature, it is a distributed model. Any attempt to nationally or globally govern any cluster of autonomous churches requires care. Local empowerment— rather than alignment to a singular overarching vision or direction—is key. Grassroots ownership of apostolic initiatives is vital. It is no threat. In fact, when apostolic immediacy is celebrated and given space to operate, the fabric of the wider coalition is preserved. It is exactly what is required for our movements to flourish!

The Bournemouth-based *Apostolic Faith Churches* governance structure prioritised the wellbeing of the overall movement over local church empowerment and autonomy. For Daniel Williams and the leaders of the

---

2 William K. Kay, *Pentecostals in Britain,* Paternoster Press, Cumbria, 2000.

Welsh congregations, the difficulties associated with breaking away from the Bournemouth group faded into insignificance when compared with the difficulty of trying to live out their apostolic calling under an approach that favoured the 'whole' over what was happening on the ground.

In 1915, many apostles became frustrated at being held back and chose to leave so they could be true to themselves. This kind of relationship breakdown is preventable when we understand the nature of apostles and what they require to flourish in their calling.

A FRUITFUL SEASON

After Daniel and the Welsh congregations reclaimed their independence, the breakaway group changed their name to the *Apostolic Church* and adopted eleven tenets of faith. Now they were free to focus on the fundamentals of evangelism and setting up communities with five-fold leadership. Through their ministry and faith, the new movement grew to over eighty assemblies with hundreds of souls being saved. Those looking on were heard to say, "We do not understand these apostolic pastors. When they visit a place, they always leave an assembly behind."

THE VALUE OF PROPHETIC DIRECTION

As a pastor, Daniel Williams was strongly influenced by the prophetic. This provided him with courage, freedom and fresh inspiration during his ministry. In his book, *The Prophetical Ministry In the Church*, Daniel concluded:

> "If we are called as an Apostolic Church to witness for something above another, we witness to the unassailable truth that we are a standing body that is an evidence of the value of the prophetic ministry.[3]"

Perhaps it was this perspective that gave him the self-confidence to offer opportunities to his colleagues and emerging church leaders, preventing him

---

3   Pastor D. P. Williams, *The Prophetical Ministry (or the Voice Gifts) In the Church,* The Apostolic Church, Penygroes, 1931.

from duplicating the Bournemouth issue under his leadership. Instead, the churches in the movement he led prospered.

GOVERNING DURING GROWTH

In 1919, other church leaders began to see what God was doing within the Apostolic Church movement, and one by one they reached out to join the group. Andrew Turnbull, who led the Burning Bush Assembly of Glasgow, brought that congregation in, along with several other churches from Scotland. Frank Hodge's assembly in Hereford also became an Apostolic Church. Three years later, a group of churches led by H.V. Chanter of Bradford was added as well[4].

Eventually, an administrative headquarters for the Apostolic Church Movement was established at Penygroes. Daniel Williams was appointed as the chief apostle, and his brother W.J. Williams was chosen to serve as the prophet of the movement. By 1930, more than one hundred and fifty churches had joined the movement in the United Kingdom. In 1933, a convention centre seating 1,250 people was built at Penygroes, and the following year a Bible school was founded[5]. A constitution and guiding principles were drawn up, and the newly centralised movement became governed by a council of apostles and prophets along with their executive team. This governance model and the formation of the constitution deeply disturbed Daniel Williams. As the leader, he saw the potential for these decisions to restrict apostolic and prophetic immediacy in the future, but despite his influence, the movement chose to proceed with a centralised approach.

---

4 William K. Kay, *Pentecostals in Britain,* Paternoster Press, Cumbria, 2000.
5 T. N. Turnbull, *What God Hath Wrought: A Short History of the Apostolic Church,* The Puritan Press, 1959.

'BELT THE GLOBE'

From the outset, The Apostolic Church Movement saw itself as a missionary movement rather than a group of churches with a 'missionary department'. These churches were characterised by evangelistic passion, fuelled by a vision to 'belt the globe' with the Gospel. In those early days, apostolic initiatives were inspired by a revelation of God's plans and purposes for particular nations. Apostles responded with appropriate strategies to fulfil these revelations. From a foundation laid by prophetic inspiration, apostolic vision and administration, many were commissioned to minister around the world. Eventually, New Zealand was embraced as part of this mandate.

3

New Zealand Touchdown

The Apostolic Church Movement's mission to 'belt the globe' achieved a significant milestone when it reached New Zealand in 1928. However, it was immigrants from the United Kingdom, rather than missionaries, who broke the ground in New Zealand. Whenever these new immigrants arrived in Wellington and met other Pentecostal believers, they naturally communicated their enthusiasm for the movement they had left behind in their homeland. Their passion for the Apostolic Church's vision was contagious, and the result was the formation of a small fellowship in that city.

The next significant development involved a man named John Hewitt, an itinerant apostolic evangelist who had relocated to Australia from Wales to help establish the Apostolic Church Movement there. On a visit to New Zealand, he encouraged Alex Wright, a leader of the emerging Apostolic fellowship in Wellington, to write a letter inviting the Apostolic Movement to New Zealand. As the head of the movement in the United Kingdom, Daniel Williams acknowledged the letter by placing a New Zealand banner among the national flags displayed in the central Apostolic church in Penygroes.

EXPANSION ACROSS THE COUNTRY

In response to the invitation from Wellington, William Cathcart, a pioneer of the Apostolic Movement in Australia, came to New Zealand. He held a series of meetings in the Concert Chamber of the Wellington Town Hall. Two hundred people attended the first meeting, and that number grew day by day. Before returning to Australia, Cathcart asked John Hewitt to come to New Zealand once more to continue the work in his place. John agreed, and invited his brother Isaac, who was also an evangelist, to come with him.

In November 1933, the two brothers held a revival and healing campaign over eight days at the Trades Hall in Wellington. Amazingly, more than a hundred people were saved. The following Sunday night they moved to the King's Theatre, where nearly seven hundred people attended. Joshua McCabe, a prophet from Scotland, joined them in the new year. On the 7th of January 1934, the Wellington church was recognised as the first official Apostolic Church in New Zealand[6]. One hundred and twelve members made up the congregation.

After the outreach in Wellington, the Hewitt brothers, Joshua McCabe, and another leader by the name of Edward Weston travelled to Nelson. Together they ministered to a group of sixty people who formed a fellowship and joined the Apostolic Church Movement. In Blenheim, ten new believers began meeting, and they joined in as well. Soon, other groups had formed in New Plymouth, Onehunga, and another in Te Kuiti. After five months of campaigns, seven Apostolic churches had been established in New Zealand[7].

ACHIEVING AUTONOMY

The following year, Alfred Greenway, an Apostolic leader from Wales, arrived as the first superintendent of the movement in New Zealand. He was a gifted teacher with a strong prophetic ministry, and under his leadership, the Apostolic Church Movement continued to grow. Through his itinerant ministry, a congregation was established in Dargaville, and in June 1935, the Hastings church was added in as well, followed by a Christchurch congregation in January 1936 and an associated service in Greymouth soon thereafter.

---

6 Brett Knowles, *Transforming Pentecostalism: The Changing Face of New Zealand Pentecostalism, 1920-2010*, Emeth Press, 2014.
7 Ibid.

That year, Frank Thompson came to New Zealand and took on the role of Acting Superintendent in place of Alfred. He later became interim president. In 1936 he opened the first purpose-built apostolic church in New Zealand, called the 'City Temple', in Lorne St, Wellington. This venue became the location for the national office and hosted an Easter convention for the next thirty-three years, an annual highlight in the life of the church. In 1937, Frank Thompson planted the Palmerston North church. During this period the Australian and New Zealand churches worked closely together, sharing ministries and resources.

During the Second World War, our churches grew, and church planting continued. The Dunedin church was started in 1942. That year, Alex Gardner, also originally from the United Kingdom, became the new president of the movement in New Zealand. With this appointment, the New Zealand church became autonomous. More than two decades later, the first New Zealand-born president, Ivor Cullen, assumed the national leadership. He led from 1965 to 1968, followed by Marcus Goulton from 1968 to 1976, and William Pearson (originally from Wales) from 1976 to 1980. James Worsfold (1980-86), John Douglas (1986-88), Ron Goulton (1988-95), Philip Underwood (1995-97) and Nick Klinkenberg (1997-2001) followed in succession.

MINISTRY TO MĀORI

From its early days, the Apostolic Movement in New Zealand had a desire to minister to the Māori people. Alfred Greenway was the first apostolic minister to reach out to the Māori, and on Labour weekend 1937, the Apostolic Māori Missioned Church was opened at Waitangi Pā in Te Puke. This became the national centre for all the Māori mission work.

Five years later, Louis Arnold was appointed as the first superintendent of the Māori Mission. The National Easter Convention was hosted by the Māori Mission on the Tūrangawaewae Marāe at Ngāruawāhia in 1979. In later years, a faction arose, and for some time, the relationship between Māori and the Apostolic Church of New Zealand as a whole became somewhat contentious. It was only after a long drawn-out court case that the topic of racial autonomy was put to rest within the movement and the issue was finally resolved.

FOREIGN MISSIONS

Papua New Guinea was one of the main mission offshoots of the early New Zealand and Australian Apostolic churches. Nearly forty New Zealanders served in Papua New Guinea in the early years and as a result of their work, hundreds of thousands of people came to know Christ, many churches were planted, and Bible colleges were established. Some would say that the effort and attention directed toward the Papua New Guinea mission meant that the church there grew at the expense of the church back home. In any case, the impact of the New Zealand Apostolic church in Papua New Guinea was significant. In 1980, a significant milestone was reached when the Papua New Guinea Apostolic church became autonomous.

WOMEN IN MINISTRY

After performing a thorough study into the role of women in ministry, a group commissioned by the council submitted their findings, and in 1992 the national movement agreed to support the ordination of women. My wife, Helen, became the first woman to be ordained. She would ultimately make her way onto a seat on the church council and then continue to serve on the National Leadership Team. We have continued to advance since then, and we can now celebrate a growing group of women being recognised, leading and bringing strong contributions at most levels of church life.

NATIONAL TRAINING

The first Apostolic Bible Training Centre in New Zealand was established by Alfred Greenway in Hamilton in 1957. Eighteen years later, a property was purchased in the Kapiti region to house the National office, and the following year, the *Te Nikau Bible College* was established on that same land in Paraparaumu, with John Douglas as the first principal. Under John's apostolic gifting, this college became one of the most crucial elements for the growth of the movement in the late 1980s and early 1990s. Over and over, the call of God was highlighted in the lives of the students, and from *Te Nikau* they were launched and equipped to step into their callings. John Douglas was key to providing a solid education for the students, and Ron Goulton as National Leader created opportunities for students to gain practical experience. The gifted group of emerging leaders who came through the college brought hope for the future of the movement in New Zealand.

4

Distress Signals

I was appointed to the Apostolic Church Council in 1981, just seven years after Helen and I had joined the Apostolic church. Having come from Anglican roots, I was learning as much as possible about the history of the movement, our emergence from the Welsh Revival, our vision to 'belt the globe', and the importance of the ascension gifts to our identity and purpose. I embraced it all, reading any and every book I could find. Even so, my appointment came as a bit of an eye-opener. I soon came face to face with human agendas as well as manipulative behaviour right at the heart of the movement for which I had grown to have such high expectations.

Without a sufficiently robust frame of reference to navigate what I encountered, there was disappointment and confusion. At the same time, I experienced a growing confidence to lead. Most of all, Helen and I were maturing and moving forward despite the things that made us uncomfortable.

THE AUCKLAND CHURCH

Then, in 1986, Helen and I received a call to pastor the Auckland Apostolic Church (later renamed, Equippers). We were excited and delighted to embrace the privilege of this role. This church already had a fifty-year history, and over time it had experienced some growth. At one high point in its history, over two hundred people regularly met together in their own building on New North Road. That was a significant congregation for a church back then. By the time we came in, however, the church had dwindled to only thirty members.

We initially struggled to turn the church around. Growth was difficult to achieve and sustain. Encountering this challenge, I turned to prayer and fasting. In seeking God's perspective on the problem, I also spent time studying the history of this local church that had become our responsibility.

We quickly realised that this church existed primarily for the movement— it had become an echo chamber, celebrating our core values among those folk already on the inside while doing little to mobilise them. The church had lost its missional edge and had an extremely limited outward focus. But that wasn't all. Like many churches, there were issues behind the scenes that had never been dealt with.

FINALLY, BREAKTHROUGH!

My time of prayer and fasting was an intense and deliberate move to seek divine strategies for breakthrough. We took our responsibility for the church very seriously, and it troubled us deeply that our initial efforts had reaped little reward.

The idea to pray and fast came from the Holy Spirit, who specifically highlighted the initial paragraphs in the book of Nehemiah to me. Nehemiah asked his brothers concerning the welfare of the city of Jerusalem, and when he received a response, the news was of such hopeless desperation that he wept, overcome with sorrow. Nehemiah mourned for many days, entering into a period of prayer and fasting. During this time, however, Nehemiah began to advance on the revelation he had received—and the impact was astounding.

The beginning of my ministry felt a little like Nehemiah's, so I readily followed his example. Like Nehemiah, I prayed for our people, confessing and repenting on their behalf for past wrongs. Out of this intercessory work, the Holy Spirit began to unlock the answers we needed. In particular, He orchestrated a meeting with a number of former Apostolic Church pastors, including some who had pastored the Auckland church. I was able to convey my concerns and frustration. In turn, every one of them readily shared, openly and humbly, about their own experiences of the church with me. We ended that meeting with united prayers of repentance and reconciliation. The atmosphere was such that you could sense God's smile over the moment!

From there, things began to shift, and forward momentum was now possible! What had been achieved through our unity in the spirit established a platform—a foundation that Helen and I were now able to build upon. New vision and fresh ideas began to flourish once more, and gradually the church began to grow.

UPSCALING OUR VISION

Our four children were teenagers at the time, so it was an easy decision for me to become the youth leader as well as the pastor. It was among the youth that we started to see salvations. Many became hungry for more and joined a weekly Bible study. We also established a Bible college so we could invest in future leadership, plus we started a creative learning school as a means to support disadvantaged youth and draw out the gifts and abilities within them. Things had turned around, and a new season had begun! Every year from that point on the church grew, primarily as people were saved and subsequently joined our number.

It was in God's heart for that church to grow beyond the city of Auckland, and the seeds for that expansion had already been planted within the heart of our community. One Tongan woman, a single mother who attended our church, and her daughter, were very dear to us. This woman started reaching out with the Gospel to all her family members, and very soon, more than fifty Tongans became followers of Jesus Christ. A large number of her family are still part of the Auckland church to this day. This experience culminated in an amazing moment later on when we were privileged to be commissioned and enabled by God to plant a church in the Kingdom of Tonga.

Another key moment undergirding our future reach as a church was a vision I received while flying domestically in New Zealand. I was reading the in-flight magazine, and as I came to the final pages, an image of the airline's flight path network was highlighted to me by the Holy Spirit. Auckland is the main hub for Air New Zealand, and along with their Star Alliance partners, their reach is global. In this image, red lines were shooting forth from Auckland to major locations around the world. As I looked, the Holy Spirit instantly superimposed an image of God preparing arrows in Auckland, people who would be slotted into God's bowstring and, in time, shot forth, curving up and away toward nations all around the world.

This apostolic vision became a major motivation for change. I started to develop a strong conviction that 'structure must serve vision', and this formed a holy discontent within me, giving me a burning in my spirit to remove everything that stood in the way of progress.

I knew God's mandate for the Auckland church was to take something that was already in the lifeblood of the Apostolic Church Movement and own it more personally. We needed to be more like a movement within a movement—a church on mission, rather than a 'church with a missions department'. From that point, the Bible college took on greater significance. I could see that it would become an important part of God's plan to train emerging leaders so they would be able to understand and carry the ethos of our mission.

HINDRANCES AND OBSTACLES

Over the years I have learnt that frustration and pressure are often God's servants to develop our faith, strengthen our conviction, teach us endurance, and bring greater clarity and ownership of the vision He has entrusted. As we progressed in line with God's global vision, the pathway was not easy, but along the way, the Holy Spirit used every obstacle to tightly align us with the details of His plan.

Our ministry in Auckland was gaining traction, but it appeared the movement we belonged to was more of a hindrance than a help. I was on the National Leadership Council, but some of the changes I wanted to bring, though obvious to me, were not seen the same way by others. At that time, I lacked the influence and authority to fix what I saw as broken. My increasing frustration with our movement's structure was not something I could remedy in isolation. So, I began to provoke the governing body, communicating the need for change however I could and whenever an opportunity presented itself.

The structure of our movement by this time had us habitually feeling like we had one hand tied behind our back. Every way we turned there was another initiative that we knew we should be implementing, but constraints on a 'movement level' hindered us. In particular, whatever resources we had raised to contribute to the church's vision were quickly centralised and then diverted elsewhere so they were unavailable to support what we had been given by the Holy Spirit to do.

One significant leader, arguing for the status quo to be maintained, summed it up by saying, "The structure we have is like 'fiscal glue' that holds our movement together." This statement was repulsive to me. I could have walked away on the spot. If that was all that was holding us together, pity help us! In that moment, I would have been happy to leave and never look back. I was prepared to start afresh without buildings, money or the like.

There were, of course, many reasons to stay. We loved our church family, and we didn't want to cause trouble for them. We understood the kind of unrest that comes when any significant leader leaves because they feel their back is against the wall. Helen and I also wanted to remain with the Apostolic Church Movement, because we held a strong desire both to belong, and to stay accountable for our beliefs, morality, and practice, having already witnessed the damage that 'lone ranger' ministry could cause.

By 1995, we were feeling like a 'thorn in the flesh' to the movement. We were torn between staying and going, and we knew this wasn't working for anyone. If we weren't careful, we knew we could develop a rebellious spirit and cause harm. I sought counsel from people outside our movement, and we consulted extensively with our core team of leaders in the Auckland church about our next steps. We came to the point where we had decided to leave. In our hearts, this was a done deal. We just needed to navigate the process.

CALLED TO STAY

Knowing that stepping down and moving on would be a challenging path to tread, I gave myself to a time of prayer and fasting. As I did, the Holy Spirit spoke to me with great clarity from my daily reading, which was in Psalm 37v3-6:

> *Trust in the Lord, and do good;* **dwell in the land,** *and* **feed on His faithfulness**. *Delight yourself also in the Lord, and He shall give you the desires of your heart. Commit your ways to the Lord,* **trust also in Him,** *and He shall bring it to pass. He shall bring forth your righteousness as light, and your justice as the noonday.*

We received this as the Holy Spirit calling us to trust Him with our future. We needed to dwell (stay) in the land (this appointed place). He was calling us to 'feed on His faithfulness' by reflecting on the goodness of God that we had experienced to date and acknowledging His care and leading in our lives thus far. He was challenging us to 'do good' by serving and giving where we had been planted.

At this time, I was also reminded of the prophetic words I had received on completing Bible college. In quick succession, one after another, five prophets had spoken directly into our situation all referencing the same verses God had already personalised for me years before:

> **Trust in the Lord** *with all your heart and lean not on your own understanding; in all your ways acknowledge Him, and He shall direct your paths.*
>
> — *PROVERBS 3:5-6*

> *Trust in the Lord, and do good;* **dwell in the land,** *and feed on His faithfulness. Delight yourself also in the Lord, and He shall give you the desires of your heart.*
>
> — *PSALM 37:3-4*

In response, we focused on delighting *ourselves* in the Lord, owning the promise that if we did so, He would give us the desires of *our* hearts. I knew that one day I would see what God had placed in my heart accomplished, and I had a growing conviction this was a path God was calling us to walk. Finally, we decided to stay in the Apostolic Movement. We had been called to trust God!

PRESSING FORWARD

Staying meant remaining in the movement. But if we were to stay, the constraints on apostles would have to go—this movement would need to enlarge its borders and release its grip! Helen and I rolled up our sleeves and reached out to those who were opposed to change, attempting to build bridges relationally so we could work together. With permission from the council leadership, I started to gather like-minded pastors from around New Zealand so we could support one another. Together we began holding leadership conferences and focused on reaching an emerging generation any way we could. I also became more aggressive in pursuing the global initiatives and ministry God had entrusted to me. From our church in Auckland, we sent a couple to London to establish a new church there. We also attempted the same in Sydney.

By now, our thinking had grown beyond a single church into what would later become the Equippers network. In connection with the Auckland church, we were able to define our vision, culture, values and mission statement. The Holy Spirit had charged us with the task of planting ten churches in ten major cities of the world, so this became our main objective. The problems in the movement were still there, but we had plenty of other things to focus on instead.

| 5

Necessary Change

At its inception, the movement in New Zealand had adopted and adapted the centralised leadership structure used by the Apostolic Church in the United Kingdom. In my mind, it was not fit for purpose because it had always inherently constrained apostolic immediacy, placing the needs of the national body before those at the coalface.

THE NATURE OF LEADERSHIP

Christ's leadership is expressed through the roles held by those with ascension ministry gifts (Ephesians 4:11). This is an important tenet of the Apostolic Church Movement and something that has been recognised since our earliest days. The focus of Ephesians 4:11 is the healthy functioning of individual local congregations and the need for diverse yet complementary leadership at that level. It does not, however, speak directly to the challenges of administering a movement. If we are to use the five-fold leadership model as a basis to administer a *movement* of local churches, we need to extract its essence, or the principles behind it.

We know that five-fold ministry is a manifestation of Christ's ministry. But what does that mean in the context of overarching structures or models? What are the principles of five-fold ministry that can enable our leadership within a church or movement? When I think about it, I see two approaches: Hierarchical governance, and servant leadership.

The most popular view of five-fold leadership is to see it as *hierarchically governmental*. Christ is the head, and His position is one of authority over us. If we understand it this way, it follows that the roles of apostle, prophet, evangelist, pastor and teacher, serve as a local expression of His 'headship'.

This was the perspective and approach the Apostolic Church Movement took historically, and ultimately this centralised form of governance was written into a constitution. Remember, this was the document that Daniel Williams was apprehensive about, the one he thought could threaten apostolic and prophetic immediacy. It turns out he was quite prophetic. With the growth our movement was now experiencing, that had certainly become the case.

HIERARCHICAL GOVERNANCE

This 'top-down' governance model was adopted in almost every country that embraced the Apostolic Church's vision—a structure that had at its highest level of authority a 'council' of recognised apostles and prophets. Of course, this was helpful when the movement was first forming, and as each nation sought to gain traction in its own right. Building identity during those birthing seasons was the greatest focus and need. Strong alignment with the vision that founders were carrying was pivotal as a basis for fledgling communities to collaborate and contribute in harmony.

As the decades rolled by and the movement scaled in each nation, an issue evolved. Degrees of separation between the central and local bodies increased until divergence of vision necessitated choices between the two groups. Eventually, the needs of the central administration were pitted against those of individual apostolic initiatives. Rather than existing as a support to nurture grassroots ideas, the apostles in authority had far too much influence and stifled new initiatives if they didn't support them. Was God providing mixed messages? Were some apostles right and others wrong? Were some apostles, with their fresh new vision, too big for their boots? No, no, and no! All of this conflict and chaos was rooted in a misunderstanding of the relationship Christ has with the church. The model was based on wrong principles, so the structure derived from it was off-kilter. Apostles were never designed to be placed over other apostles. Any governance structure in the church that is pitched this way has missed the point. It may be tactical at times, but it will never be strategic.

Christian leadership is not hierarchical. It always presents as servant leadership that nurtures, supports, provides and encourages by coming under another to release them. The greatest among us must be the least. There is another way to govern and administer a movement that still holds the ascension gifts near and dear. To find it, we need to turn everything upside down, empowering apostles, prophets, evangelists, pastors and teachers to bring breakthrough and do the equipping, while establishing *elders* to bring covering and governance.

PROBLEMS ON THE GROUND

This distinction between 'top-down' and 'bottom-up' leadership is more than theoretical, because how you define Christ's delegated role has a practical impact on the day-to-day decision-making and management of resources. Whatever your governance model, it will be administered correspondingly.

In the Apostolic Church Movement, the council in each country appointed one person to be the national leader (formerly called the president). They also appointed an executive team of around seven people, all of whom were apostles. This group was responsible for the day-to-day operations of the national movement, and they were also the legal trustees of the registered Trust. In New Zealand, this was called the 'Apostolic Church Trust Board' and all the properties owned throughout the country were held in and managed out of this entity. Every pastor's salary was set by the council, and these were also administered by the National Office. To illustrate how centralised and controlling this became, local churches in those early days had to submit payments and payment requests to the national office, even for something as insignificant as the purchase of a new toilet. Thankfully, this had begun to shift, and churches were able to retain a portion of their offerings for local administration by the time I was elected as National Leader. However, salaries and buildings were still controlled nationally because a local church pastor was seen as a staff member of the national body.

DOWNSIDES OF HIERARCHICAL LEADERSHIP

In reality, the Apostolic Church was one church nationally with many branches, and the council ran the whole thing. A local church was encouraged to appoint elders for local spiritual matters and to oversee local administration, but these elders were powerless when it came to governance. The ultimate authority still rested with the National Executive and Council, who held complete legal responsibility and control.

Apostles were appointed based on their ability and willingness to contribute and align to a national vision rather than because they demonstrated the grace of apostleship—the ability to receive and steward vision in their own right—through their ministry. This eroded the role of apostles within our movement nationally and watered down the effectiveness of their leadership in general. In short, both the role of an apostle and a local apostle's freedom to follow through on their vision was compromised, effectively crippling apostolic function. The movement had essentially become apostolic in name only.

This stifled rather than promoted good leadership. Only compliant pastors could survive, but they didn't have the aptitude or talent to cultivate significant growth or steward breakthrough. For a movement that prided itself on apostolic and prophetic ministry, there was a distinct lack of strategic action and thriving new initiatives. Church planting was more like church 'plonking' because new churches were not emerging from the ministry of a visionary apostolic leader. Newly established churches were treated more like street kids bundled into an orphanage than children nurtured at home in the care of their parents and then launched into life properly.

The results were consistent with that imagery. Many new churches experienced a distinct failure to thrive and ended up dying or closing. Apostles who were appointed on a flawed basis developed a false sense of security and an over-inflated view of their own importance. It was obvious to anyone looking on that this approach was never going to work, so much so that certain observers outside of our movement found many of the appointments ridiculous.

Beyond our movement, I could see flourishing ministries that were apostolic in vision and doing well. I compared their situation to ours and concluded, to my discouragement, that those people and what they were doing would never have survived in our environment. Genuine apostolic visionaries need to be given the freedom to create just enough structure to serve their Holy Spirit-inspired vision. If administrative autonomy is not provided, the compulsion to leave becomes almost irresistible. We had already felt that dynamic, and we could see it in the lives and ministries of many who were in leadership around us. When one significant leader left the movement, along with his church, I felt that enough was enough. I distilled my thinking onto paper and submitted a proposal to the Council outlining a vision for change. Something needed to be done!

MOUNTING FRUSTRATION

Some changes resulted from all my provocation, and that was encouraging to me. This strengthened my conviction that something could be done, even though the current national leader had told me he was happy with the status quo and didn't see any need for reforms. It began to dawn on me that a significant shift was necessary.

Appointments to lead the movement nationally came around every two years. I put my name forward twice to become the National Leader—once in 1997, and again in 1999. Though unsuccessful, we were committed to staying, and I knew I was obliged to take every opportunity to make things better. But knowing we couldn't and wouldn't walk away added to my frustration rather than alleviating it. We were accommodated, but by no means celebrated, stuck in a dysfunctional environment bursting with unrealised vision that would have challenged our faith even in a perfect system.

CULTURAL REFORMATION

6

A Mandate to Lead

After nearly ten years on the council, my vision for the future of our movement had become fully formed, and I knew we had no choice but to make structural changes. What existed inhibited breakthrough. Without the ability to leap forward in innovative ways, we would be stifled by every challenge we faced. We needed to create an environment for apostolic initiatives to be freely pursued. But beyond that, there was more to do. The vision I carried was three-fold. As well as enabling apostolic immediacy, we needed to make way for emerging generations, and we needed a kingdom-focused culture.

EMERGING GENERATIONS

In my mind, it was essential that we facilitate younger people to move up and take their place in leadership. I wanted a culture that encouraged emerging generations and created a supportive environment where they could thrive. In our Auckland City church, this meant older generations working with those rising up in leadership, getting behind their ideas, and championing their priorities.

Movements begin with a vital sense of engagement. There is a real freshness and a vibrancy about what is happening that resonates with the culture of the day and speaks to the deep longings within the heart of an emerging generation. To maintain our connectedness and relevance, we need a continual cycle of refreshing. Without it, we will become stale and unable to sustain a significant contribution.

Music is a clear example of this. It can be a temptation for leaders to stay with what is known and all that has been traditionally life-giving, rather than creating an environment in worship where the younger generation can encounter God alongside their peers. By creating an accessible and relevant atmosphere for the younger generation, we make room for them to thrive. What better way to create a legacy than to welcome them in and give them a running start so they can replace us as champions of what God is doing? They become part of a continuum so that what we have established continues to thrive and grow. And then, when the time comes, we are able to confidently step aside and make room for them to rise into their leadership potential.

KINGDOM FOCUS

Kingdom focus has an essential role in safeguarding our community as an answer to a broken world. It requires everyone in the movement to be equipped so that they can step confidently into their God-given assignment. This can only happen when apostolic leaders are released and we have made room for the emerging generations.

Education is key! How do we discover our calling? What does it mean to bring the kingdom to a particular industry or part of society? Is it possible to flourish as agents of God's kingdom in a world that often runs counter to His values? We begin by training our people to understand, exemplify and live out kingdom culture wherever they are needed. We create a dynamic that gathers people close, unpacks their destiny, and subsequently sends them out on assignment in whichever sphere of life the Holy Spirit directs them.

MY SERVANT, MONK

It was one thing to carry this vision, but without the scope to outwork it, this had become more of a 'burning in my bones' than a joy. Additionally, the call to stay made very real the problems within the movement. For now, the issues my vision could have addressed were ours to experience—and to own, as well. We felt the tension, but we also felt the promise, the sense that my three-fold vision would eventually be realised.

In the meantime, Helen and I had moved to London to lead the church there, which we renamed 'Equippers'. For us, this was entirely an exercise in obedience. Although we had carried the vision to plant churches internationally for some time, leaving New Zealand had never been in our plans.

From London, I had regularly returned to New Zealand to visit the Auckland church and attend council meetings. This time, however, I was coming back for an election council, knowing that the previous leader would not be standing for re-election. It was fairly certain that I would be nominated for the role. If I was successfully elected as national leader, this would present a great opportunity to finally outwork the vision I had been carrying for so long. However, the call to London had been so clear that returning to New Zealand to do so, felt inappropriate. Feeling no inclination to compromise on our mission in the United Kingdom, I flew back to New Zealand unsure of how it would all turn out.

When we came together as a Council, I was soon asked if I would be willing to serve as national leader. I agreed, but only on the terms in which I foresaw this working. At the time, the role of national leader was seen more as a 'pastor of pastors', with the national leader travelling around the churches in New Zealand, encouraging the local pastors. My vision was for something different. In my mind, my job would be to guide the movement. For that, I didn't need to be based in New Zealand. I was willing to create and oversee a team of leaders remotely from London. This would have never worked if I had seen the role as being a pastor of pastors, but I didn't.

Three candidates were being considered for the appointment that day, and this led to some good debate. There were a lot of strong minds and strong views in the room as the council discussed their alternatives. In the midst of the deliberations, Tony Faitala, a lovely man and a recognised prophet of Niuean descent, stood to his feet. He was brief and to the point. "My servant

Monk is the man," he said, and then he sat down. The council responded by judging this word to determine whether it was of God. They concluded that because the speaker was not politically involved and had not consulted with anyone beforehand, it came from revelation. It was therefore judged to be a prophetic word.

The Council then asked if I would consider changing my mind about where we were based. I thought it over before giving my response, but I still didn't feel that Helen and I should walk away from our London assignment. I communicated this to the council and shared my plan, stating, "If elected, I would lead the movement strategically from the United Kingdom. I wouldn't take an income for the initial period, and I would cover the cost of two of the four return flights that would be necessary in outworking this role."

This proposal would allow me to facilitate strategic meetings, attend the national conference, and participate in the National Leadership Tour during my first year. I explained that I was confident that, using this approach, I could and would outwork my three-fold vision.

The elections generally work by consensus rather than by vote, and the Council had been trying to work toward that. When I finished talking, there was widespread agreement in the room about this motion. That was the miracle in this whole situation. Our staying overseas had presented an unfamiliar challenge, which the council had come to terms with. It seemed to me a God-ordained moment. I had received a mandate, primarily from God, but also from the Council.

Anointed leadership is paramount if you want to change a culture. Others can help, but no one can carry it quite the same as the leader who is entrusted with the vision. I left that meeting knowing I needed to step firmly into my new role as national leader of the Apostolic Church Movement in New Zealand. The movement needed me to bring a fresh inspiring view of our future as well as an understanding of the next steps we would need to take together. I was aware of the concentric circles of influence. First, I needed to get the National Leadership Team on board with the vision, and I intended to use our National Leadership Tour to foster buy-in among the regional leaders. Then, through our annual conferences, I hoped to seed change within the wider community.

I was determined to have the confidence required to execute my vision. I didn't have to be the greatest preacher, but I needed to publicly communicate my vision, to make it my business to voice it at every opportunity because God had appointed me to change the direction of the movement.

THE NATIONAL LEADERSHIP TEAM

From the outset, I knew that the entire movement's ethos needed to change. Our top-down leadership style supported pastoral leaders, not apostolic leaders. But the Council and the National Leadership Team were difficult to lead. Their robust opinions did not necessarily align with my own, but that was where the strongest voices were, and the influence they carried within the movement made working with them entirely worth the effort. Though our conversations were a bit chaotic at times, I had a godly confidence in my role, and the Council respected my mandate to lead.

"We have become stale," I argued. "Are you going to join me in rectifying that?" It was a simple invitation. Elections were held biannually, which meant that every two years I needed to present a refreshed vision and communicate our progress in a way that was sufficient for the Leadership Team to provide me with additional time to get the job done. From the start, I gave it my all. I figured that if at any point the Leadership Team didn't like the direction we were taking, they could—and would—vote me out.

We focused on changing our culture through our annual conference and our National Leadership Tour. At first, there was a level of pushback, as there always is when we disrupt the status quo.

The resistance from those opposed to the direction I was taking things, was unfortunately directed largely against our own apostolic initiative, which Helen and I called 'Equippers'. By the time I was appointed to the role of National Leader, we had become a vibrant and successful network. In a short space of time, churches had begun joining in, and some of them had taken the name Equippers. Unlike most Apostolic Churches, we were attracting young people, and not everybody knew what to make of this. One person on the National Leadership Team went as far as to say, "Equippers has the appearance of evil."

With progressive leadership, challenges are constant, but they don't need to be crippling. The added pressure should instead strengthen our resolve. I recognised the pushback for what it was and determined not to take things too personally. My constant prayer was that the Holy Spirit would give me tough skin and a soft heart.

THE CONFERENCES

Annual conferences have always been an important occasion for the Apostolic Movement in New Zealand. In the early years of my leadership, I would often look across the audience at our annual conference and notice that only half of the attendees seemed connected to what was going on. The rest seemed distracted and unengaged.

Our approach was to remain unrelenting in our desire for the presence of God. Only He could truly unite us around the vision I was carrying and turn it from *my* vision into *our* vision, and ultimately into *our* reality.

The culture of a movement is shaped and often defined by its music. At first, we brought in worship leaders from outside our movement to lead worship at our annual conferences, but it was somewhat disjointed—the style and flavour of worship kept changing and wasn't always contributing to the journey we needed to go on. I made the decision to invite Wayne and Libby Huirua, well-known and widely respected worship leaders from our church in Auckland, to take over the leadership of the worship team at our national conferences. This was one of several important partnerships that built continuity and supported us in creating the culture we needed.

I led the speaking at the national conferences, and Helen would often take a session as well. Helen has always been a good teacher, capable in front of a crowd, and highly respected well before the voice of women became stronger in our movement. In that regard, she led the way, spearheading the direction we felt God directing us to go in. We also brought in some great communicators—speakers who would come into the room with the sensitivity to pick up on what was needed. Somehow, we got the right speakers at just the right time, and they were able to help us set the culture and consolidate our position. Danny Guglielmucci from Edge Church in Adelaide was one such speaker. He was very capable, coming alongside us as a partner to edge us forward in the right direction.

I always prayed and fasted before going into meetings like that, and praise God, He heard and answered our prayers. God put on me—and others who needed it at the time—the capacity and tenacity to do all that was needed to accomplish His purposes in those environments. More importantly, He came through for us with the anointing at those conferences, visiting us with some strategic moments that moved the dial for us and shifted the atmosphere.

Our annual conferences were becoming transformative to the wider culture. For me, a highlight came five years into my leadership. Looking across the audience, I noticed ninety to ninety-five percent of the audience were fully engaged in the worship and the presence of God. "Okay, now we're winning," I thought. It was an incredible moment.

THE LEADERSHIP TOUR

The Leadership Tour was also a powerful opportunity to influence the trajectory of the movement. Once a year, the five or so members of the National Leadership Team took to the road for a week, bringing pastors together in Dunedin, Christchurch, Wellington, Rotorua and Auckland. These weeks were intense! We'd arrive at one of the city churches at 10 a.m., meet with the regional leaders and pastors until 3 p.m., then we'd have a meal together, followed by a night meeting.

Every apostolic pastor was expected to attend, along with their elders and their up-and-coming leaders if possible. Day after day, the National Leadership Team were up front, sharing the vision and connecting with leaders who in turn would take information and revelation back to their people. It was very, very successful.

Every pastor had the opportunity to meet us in person, engage in conversation, question what we were doing—or how we were doing things—and raise any issues they were facing. It also gave us time to talk things through properly with individual pastors.

One of the important early changes was our decision to move toward relational networks rather than geographical networks with regional leaders. This was particularly relevant when senior leaders were choosing overseers to work with them on behalf of the movement. We began to encourage our leaders to embrace the close connections they had made with other leaders, regardless of how near or far they were geographically. This immediately led to more comfortable working relationships because they were organic relationships built on trust that had already been established.

We also encouraged the churches toward autonomy. Initially, this was poorly understood. We were not asking churches to adopt the attitude of, 'no one tells us what to do' or to develop an unhealthy spirit of independence. We simply wanted them to take responsibility for governing their own affairs, while remaining under the covering of a movement supervisor.

Ian Wright, one of our National Leadership Team members who accompanied us on these tours, helped us significantly through these changes, coming in at critical points to help break down barriers in people's thinking. Nick Klinkenberg, the former national leader, also contributed greatly, as did Manu Pohio, one of our Indigenous leaders. Our son Sam was also part of the tour. His gifting and influence with the youth had earned him a position on the National Leadership Team, and he presented a couple of outstanding sessions. Everybody who heard him agreed that his voice was essential to the future of our movement.

We were making good progress as a team, but it didn't take long for nagging factional issues to surface which created real difficulties for us from a leadership perspective.

7

Factional Friction

One year into my appointment, I was enjoying a meal in London with some friends from America. That night, two of the men who I have since come to know very well, took me aside from the group and prophesied saying, "God is calling you and strengthening you to take down a 'goliath', a strong spirit that is hindering what He wants to accomplish in the nation."

This was amazing, considering we had been introduced only as pastors of the church there in the United Kingdom. These men did not know my situation or even my role in New Zealand. Nevertheless, they could not have been more on the mark.

Throughout my sixteen years of leading the movement, we were conscious of the spiritual warfare involved in what we were doing. The 'goliath' they spoke of was a political and religious spirit, causing people to be controlled and keeping them from becoming who God had called them to be. This often manifests as *institutionalism*—but whatever we call it, it is characterised by a loss of freedom to dream, to 'breathe' and to explore what God is placing on our hearts.

CULTURAL AUTONOMY

But there was another challenge that had both physical and spiritual components, and it threatened our core identity as a united group of people travelling together as a movement under God. The Apostolic Church in

New Zealand traditionally had favour with Indigenous and other cultural groups, and it was important to us that they were properly represented within the movement. Some members of these cultural groups already sat on the Council, and in the years prior to my appointment, a sub-council had also been established alongside the main Apostolic Council to ensure cultural concerns were taken into account as part of our decision-making.

I was encouraging people to pursue the vision they carried and seeking to empower freedom of expression and diversity at a grassroots level. But over time, factional thinking developed which had the opposite effect, and what could have been life-giving was perceived as a threat. In response, the sub-council asked for an allocation of finances that they could hold and use independently, while still being able to use the Apostolic Church name. Agreeing to this would have meant we had two councils and essentially two movements rather than one, placing us in a situation where divergence was inevitable and fairly irreversible. We would also construct a level of financial dependence that coupled together an unbalanced and unsustainable alliance, setting both councils up for a permanent state of tension.

When we come together we have access to each other's strengths, but isolating ourselves invites problems. The Council had previously faced administrative difficulties when representatives of the cultural faction had applied for and received funding, but unfortunately, no records whatsoever had been kept of the spending. We as trustees were accountable for what had happened to it, but there was nothing we could do to track the expenditure as we normally would. We were operating as a trust and were transparent in our financial considerations and dealings across the board, but the necessary structures to delegate that responsibility had not yet been implemented.

The structures we eventually put in place provided all the financial autonomy this group craved, but with accountability spread over a wider group of people so there was no alternative but to steward the finances well. These days we have achieved a good solution for everyone involved, but it was some time coming.

CHALLENGES AND INTIMIDATION

For more than twenty years, we lived with some level of unease with the cultural faction. At one point when the cultural faction voiced their requests, we had to make a clear call. I resisted what they were asking for, which caused frustration. When certain members within this group tried to intimidate me, one of their older spiritual leaders thankfully stepped in and said, "Stop! You are out of order."

In that moment, I felt for this dissenting group. We were all simply trying to breathe within the structure we had inherited, and it was hard on us all. But I was graced to see the bigger picture, while they struggled to see beyond the situation they found themselves in. It was my responsibility to look across the whole movement, speak to the needs of *all* the groups, and lead a united whole rather than standing by as we splintered into pieces.

This particular problem, which mostly centred on assets, was not dissimilar to what was being faced by all the leaders on the ground within our movement. The purse strings were controlled centrally, and that was generally disempowering. I was set on fixing that for *everyone*, but I wanted to build genuine autonomy. That was not what this group was proposing, and most of all, it was not an expression of kingdom values.

At a grassroots level, these types of issues tend to sort themselves out organically. But as soon as they become politicised, things can get heated. People begin talking about privilege and entitlement, the premise being that some have an advantage over others and will always be better off. This makes it more likely for competition to creep in, and then the situation becomes divisive.

That was always my concern. When we get to heaven we will be one people worshipping God, and I'm convinced we should not be dividing along racial lines in the here and now. It is possible to come together from all over the world, yet share the same kingdom vision, values and culture. As a leader within our movement, there was a constant temptation to actively blend cultural leadership with the church. In my mind, we need to resist the impulse to mix ethnic culture with kingdom culture. What we are building in line with the Word of God is at a level beyond national cultures and human ideals.

RECONCILIATION COURT

The desire to divide along racial lines had been around for many years, and it wasn't going away. Instead, tensions had risen around the ownership of a church building in Rotorua. We weren't passionate about holding onto the building, but it had been invested in by the movement in the years before the people we were dealing with had arrived in Rotorua. Knowing its historical value to the wider movement, we didn't want to just give the whole property away to one particular leader and his faction without some acknowledgement of what others had contributed financially to the building's existence. As a council, we weren't trying to be headstrong about anything. We were ready to negotiate and work through the issues, but those on the other side seemed intent on fighting for their rights and entitlements.

We had already spent countless hours on this dispute. The National Leadership Team had also engaged a lawyer, and by now, we had spent over a hundred thousand dollars in legal fees. This was so frustrating to me because it felt like such a waste of money. One day I was praying and expressing my frustration to God about this issue. "This is ridiculous!" I said to God, "What are we doing here?" Immediately, the Holy Spirit spoke a clear word to me. I heard Him say, "David's battles were not cheap." That settled it for me. "Okay," I thought. "This is the cost of doing business. We've just got to get on and do this."

Very soon after this, things came to a head. A complaint was brought against us, and it went to court. I was in London when we received the summons, and I flew back for the hearing. I had never been in a courthouse before, so this was a new experience for me. I remember how daunting it felt as I walked through the glass doors of the High Court in Auckland.

This was a reconciliation court, which meant that the judge's goal was to bring a resolution to both parties and help us reach an agreement. When he realised that both sides were from the same church movement, the judge remarked, "This is a Christian grievance, so rather than a judgment, we will try and bring reconciliation."

Unlike a regular court case, we all sat around a table to present our material. Our lawyer had employed an advisor who understood how the church operated, which had helped in the preparation of our case. On the day of the court case, however, our lawyer became sick and sent an associate to take his place. When it came time to present our case, the associate spoke for a few minutes, then turned to me and said, "Okay, Bruce, you can continue." I just presumed the lawyer would do all the talking, so I was very surprised, but in the moment, I figured, "I've never done this before, but I'm the man to do it," and I rolled with it. I turned to the associate and asked him, "Is my tie straight?"—then I stood up and went for it!

In the end, the judge brought both parties to an agreement where the dissenting faction was required to cover all of our court costs. This faction separated from the movement at that point, but they received a section of land next door to the building (which had been held by the Trust until then), and we were able to retain the building within the movement. At that point, there was a natural parting, but the factional issues were defused. We were no longer fighting this battle.

8

Despised to Desired

In my view, the Apostolic Movement in New Zealand lost its way very early on in its history. I remember, even as a kid, my father laughing at the Apostolic Church. He referred to them as "a funny little group that were very insular". By now, however, we had become a bit despised. Other groups, like the Assemblies of God, were gaining traction. They had grown in recent years, and we hadn't. We had planted a few new churches, but people looked at our 'ministry gift' theology—especially our take on the apostolic gift—and laughed, because we had institutionalised it. They could point to many of our leaders and justifiably say, "That person's not an apostle, and neither is that one . . ."

As a result, we had developed a bit of an inferiority complex. We had become introspective and self-conscious to the point where it was difficult for us to focus on what we had been given to do. Helen picked up on the fact that we were very much on the back foot, and she encouraged me: "Let's deliberately speak into this perception. This mindset needs to change." I agreed, and over the next few weeks we thought together about the challenge this presented and shared scriptures until I had a razor-sharp focus on the breakthrough we needed.

HELEN'S MESSAGE

Another annual conference was approaching, and when our guest minister for this significant event cancelled, I saw it as an opportunity for Helen and me to minister into the heart of our movement. On the first night of the conference, I preached a sermon I called 'Shut the Doors', taken from the words Elisha spoke to the widow with the jar of oil in 2 Kings 4:4. In response to the prophet's instruction, the widow shut the doors to her house and focused on the jars *inside* the house. The message I preached was that our people were vessels that could and did carry incredible anointing and giftings. We needed to esteem what the Holy Spirit had entrusted to us as a movement. We needed to champion our own heroes of faith!

Helen resounded with a strong prophetic message called, 'Moving from Despised to Desired'. She reflected on the current state of the movement and articulated that although we had become despised, God had a path back for us. Preaching from Ezekial 36, Helen traced the journey of God's people from 'despised' to 'desired'. Over their years in exile, they had been the object of ridicule, but that was not their destiny. Their ruins would be rebuilt, and their cities would become habitable again. Instead of a public eyesore and a barren waste of space, the desolate land would be cultivated once more. Like Sunset Boulevard, an area that was naturally quite barren could be transformed by people who believed it could become a great place to live. Helen reminded us that we could work toward our movement being a place that was attractive, a desirable place where people would grow and flourish, where gifts and initiatives would be released—so much so that others would 'look over the fence' as they did in Ezekiel 36, and marvel at the transformation.

Helen preached that transformation comes when we understand the value God attaches to us and remember that we have great worth in His eyes. So, how could we align ourselves to Christ's assessment of us? How could we ready ourselves to align with His vision and participate fully in His purpose for us? In Helen's mind, it came down to acknowledging our lack and seeking Jesus to fill us as His vessels with dreams and desires—not only for ourselves but for the world around us. "We can't be inspirational to others if we are trapped in negative hopeless mindsets toward ourselves," she said.

In her sermon, Helen reassured us that the vulnerability and embarrassment, fear and shame, and of course the lack of energy that emanates from feeling hopeless, were not going to be the end of our story. There was much to rise above, and our current situation did not and would not define our future. We needed to keep moving, because a better reality lay ahead, just a little further down the road.

Helen spoke about some research that was performed by a psychologist by the name of Richard Wiseman. His findings revealed that 'unlucky' people have mindsets that blind them to the opportunities right in front of their eyes. Because they expect things to be hard, they miss the chance to enjoy things that are easier. Helen explained that in order to move forward, mindsets would need to change. We would need self-respect—hope and expectation as a community—if we were to move from a despised reality to a desired one.

Referring to the story in 2 Kings 4, Helen showed how the widow demonstrates a valuable pattern. This woman was in a destitute and despised situation—she was a widow, *and* the creditor was on his way to take her two sons away and into slavery. Elisha spoke into her circumstance saying,

> "Go, borrow vessels from everywhere, from all your neighbours –
> empty vessels; do not gather just a few. And when you have come in,
> you shall shut the door behind you and your sons; then pour it into
> all those vessels, and set aside the full ones."
>
> — 2 KINGS 4:4

And that is what she did. She took the little oil that she had and filled one jar after another until every vessel was filled. It was only then that the oil finally ran out. When the widow told Elisha what had happened, he said, "Go, sell the oil and pay your debt, and you and your sons live on the rest" (v. 7). Her obedience transformed her situation from *despised* to *desired*. She was privileged to have a resource to sell at a time when scarcity was the norm. The widow had plenty to be frustrated about but she went to the right source, refusing to allow anxiety, depression, panic or worldly thinking to have authority in her life. She heard the prophet asking, "Tell me, what do you have in the house? What is there to work with?" (v. 2) and she began to attach value to what she *already had!*

"God has deposited seeds of greatness and potential within us," Helen declared. "They are latent and can't be multiplied unless we pick them up, believe in our God-given grace, and sow bountifully." Just as Elisha had said to the widow, "Do not gather just a few," and a demonstration of obedience was required of the widow, the same was required of us. It was no small thing for the widow to go to all her neighbours asking for jars, but like the widow, we had to be willing to give it our all and put ourselves out there! "God can't bless us beyond our embarrassment," Helen relayed. "That was true for her then, and it's true for us now. As the widow filled each vessel she was giving God something to work with. He put His 'supernatural' into her 'natural', and as a result, she had an answer for her creditors. The same is true for us!"

Then she began to speak directly into our situation. "How can this simple story be a pattern for us as a movement? How can we move from being despised to desired, just as the widow did? We need to believe in the God-given gifts among us. Our people are our jars to fill! We need to identify every empty vessel among us, every person that God wants to fill and use. He requires us to close the doors and focus within for a time, promising that He will give us what we need to fill those vessels. As we do so, we will gather strength within our ranks and move from being despised to being desired. As we set apart each full vessel, we believe that what we possess as a movement will become an answer for every challenge that will ever come knocking on our door. We will be partnering with God to safeguard the future of our movement."

LIFTING OUR VOICES

Helen's prophetic gift was useful in locating where we were at, and her message at the conference brought the revelation needed to move us forward into transformation. As a movement, we leaned into it. We began to nurture leadership talent within our walls instead of looking outside of ourselves. The following year, we focused on honouring the leadership within the Apostolic Movement. That seeded a breakthrough season for us. We began to change our culture and celebrate what God was doing among us, instead of focusing on other great moves of God such as Hillsong and others. We started lifting our own people, highlighting our own voices! Together we were building language and thinking that would be pivotal to the movement in New Zealand later on.

Leadership is mostly about communication, and the language we use is massively important. How we describe and talk about things is pivotal if vision and ideas are to take root. As we pushed in the direction the Holy Spirit was indicating, additional language came, and we began to talk about 'raising up heroes from within'.

Across our churches, we sat down and said, "Come on. Let's lift up some of the voices. We've got great prophets—let's start to respect the prophetic mantle. Our current model is constrictive to prophets, so let's open that up so they can operate freely. We have a solid group of young people coming through. Let's lift up the voices of the emerging generation. Let's listen to their ideas and come in behind them. They are the future, and they can break open the culture around us."

One of the voices we celebrated was that of Ian Wright. Ian is a comedian preacher with the ability to crack you up and then crack you open so God can do His deep work. He and I worked well together because I was intense, and he was the opposite. He would have the entire room in fits of laughter. His humour got everyone's guard down so their hearts were exposed, ready to be ministered to. He was great at creating environments where we could pray for people, and things would shift for them. On leadership tours, I would often teach in the morning and then put him on after lunch. He would break the intensity, something which was so necessary for some of the conversations we were having.

The other thing we did was bring those with a gift of teaching to the fore so they could be heard. One of our teachers from Dunedin, Stan Shaw, gave a phenomenal sermon about the nature of good apostolic leadership. He based his teaching on 1 Corinthians 4:1, and in particular, explained that the word 'servant' in the original language of Ancient Greek (*huperetes*) alluded to the bottom level of rowers in a Roman galley. His point was that apostolic leadership is not about being at the top of the structure, but that we should function as 'under-rowers'. The principles Stan Shaw unpacked in that sermon have since become embedded deeply within our movement.

WHAT IS LEADERSHIP?

This concept of apostolic 'under-rowers' also shaped my understanding of my role as an apostle within the movement. As apostles, we can bring breakthrough, but we need the prophets to show the way forward and the teachers to provide understanding. We need emerging leaders to gift us with insight so that we can meet their peers where they are to be found culturally. As apostolic leaders, we had an obligation to ensure everyone heard those voices. We could affirm what they were saying and act on it, creating a 'scaffold' so that the whole group could build on those perspectives together.

The paradox of leadership is that we must oversee in terms of responsibility, but we must come under those we lead in order to accomplish things. We are to be under-rowers. We expend effort and create momentum, but we need to carry that with humility if we are ever going to reflect Christ, the personification of servant leadership. We must be in the business of not taking ourselves too seriously and be very ready to lift others up. An apostle's primary function is not governance, it is breakthrough.

This had implications for our leadership across the board. To solve some of our fundamental and structural problems, we would need to flip our leadership model upside down. Traditionally we had talked about five-fold leadership as the 'headship' gifts. We don't call them that anymore. Instead, we began using the term 'Ascension Ministry Gifts'—gifts given to the church after Christ ascended to heaven. This alternative way of speaking about the five-fold gifts transformed our ability to walk in those gifts and empowered us to lead with a healthy attitude toward others.

This demonstrates a cascading effect. In our case, the story starts with a single leader—an *apostle* appointed with a vision in hand. A *prophet* at his side reveals a mindset of being 'despised' that needs to be challenged so the movement can progress in realising the vision. We begin fostering and championing leadership from within and lifting up our own voices. We start celebrating our own, and as we do, a *teacher* redefines leadership for us. In so doing, he provides us with the 'shape' of the structural change necessary to realise the original vision.

The result was no small change in thinking for us. This was a move away from a traditional tenet of apostolic theology that had endured for a hundred years. We had always believed that church government was by apostles, prophets, teachers, evangelists, teachers, elders and deacons, and there was a belief that these tenets could not and should not be changed. But more and more, the major change points were coming from people within our movement, and momentum was growing as a result. Most importantly, we were keeping in step with what we were hearing from the Holy Spirit.

BECOMING DESIRED

We had challenged the factional issues, the mindset we operated with, and the very basis of our theology. Now I needed to challenge the political spirit in our organisation that demanded key leaders have a platform session at the conference. "Why?" I asked. "How does bringing every leader onto the stage serve our vision?" Our leaders were here to serve, not to be part of a parade. Servant leadership became a key value for us. The ultimate compliment, especially when travelling in ministry, was for a pastor to say to us, "Thank you. You served us well." This value of servant leadership became incredibly important later on in Europe where people were used to either top-down centralised bureaucracies or independent churches. Bringing a strong gift to lift people up rather than control them has led to many leaders wanting to connect with our movement.

This leadership perspective also enabled us to make room for emerging voices. Soon we were able to bring younger people into key positions of leadership where they could speak into how we could be more relevant. Among them, our son Sam's voice became increasingly important. As a movement, we were starting to be celebrated outside of ourselves. Recognising that something had changed for us, other church and movement leaders began inviting our people to speak at their events. Esther Greenwood, one of our Pacifica leaders with a gift of preaching was invited to lead and speak at major youth conferences. Jordan Smith, a key communicator from our Auckland team, also began to have a voice outside of our movement. I started getting wider invitations as well. It soon became abundantly clear that as we had followed the Lord, we had experienced a dramatic shift. We had moved from being despised to being desired.

9

Spurious Glue

One thing I've learnt is you can't change culture quickly. It takes time because mindsets need to shift, and to succeed properly you need to also see transference from one generation to another. The slow and challenging work to win the hearts and minds of those who are older and comfortable with the status quo eventually gives way once a critical mass begins to own it deeply and it becomes a new normal for the community. This happens at a point when the change we are stewarding begins resonating with the next generation.

Our journey to transformation was over many years, taking one step at a time and incrementally embedding points of freedom and areas of empowerment. This was especially true in the area of our movement's financial management.

It was a significant step forward when we agreed to give local churches the right to establish their own legal identity so that they could operate somewhat autonomously. Before that, we operated as a single centralised trust. All salaries were paid from the National Office, and a lot of the administration was managed there too. Each church had a financial code and a bank account so transactions could be tracked, but everything was owned and operated by the National Office.

The Auckland City Church was the first natural adopter of this new way of operating. We established our own Trust, but the movement was the settler of the trust, so they had ultimate authority over our affairs. This fell short of all I thought we needed, but it was still a welcome change. Now we were able to employ who we wanted, pay our staff's salaries, and administer our affairs in ways that worked best for us as a church.

COMBATING MINDSETS

Having its own entity enabled us to plot a course for Auckland City Church to a greater degree. However, because we were essentially operating as 'a trust within a trust', there was the continual risk that a veto from the Council could derail our expression of the Holy Spirit-given vision we carried and hamstring our efforts to be true to our calling at a grassroots level. This 'veto power' had been written into a revised version of the Partnership Manual for the movement, and it reflected the mindset held by a proportion of the Council at the time, especially two of the members who wanted to ensure fixed assets such as buildings were never given away to local church trusts. "The assets are the fiscal glue that holds us together," one of them remarked. I found that statement appalling and thought to myself when I heard it, "If that's all that holds us together, we are in real trouble." That way of thinking persisted for years, and it took a radical change in trust law by the government for us to eventually break free from it.

In the meantime, establishing our own trust as the Auckland church was a win, if only a small one. What surprised me was the lack of other churches taking advantage of these new freedoms available to them. Of all the churches in the movement, the Auckland City Church led the change and another church soon followed suit, but over the next four or five years few others did the same. This extremely slow uptake of the new trust structures convinced me of one thing—in New Zealand, we were a pastoral rather than an apostolic movement. If we had been apostolic in flavour, bursting with vision that demanded swift realisation on the ground, we would have been clamouring to adopt the advantages of the new structures as quickly as possible.

With this adjustment to the partnership manual, elders were empowered to run their own churches, manage their own staffing and salaries, and administer their affairs in ways that made sense to them with what they were attempting to achieve. Instead of paying all their income into centrally owned bank accounts, they now kept a fair proportion back for the local church to use and paid a levy to the movement. In the Auckland church, we did what we taught as the 30-30-30-10 principle—after we'd paid our levy, we allocated thirty percent to staff salaries, thirty percent to administration, thirty percent to buildings, and ten percent toward our mission. The levy was initially uncomfortably high (gradually we were able to reduce this to a reasonable percentage (~5%) and we capped the levy so no churches pay more than ~$18k), but at least leaders were now able to make some adjustments locally. This enabled them to employ the right people for the task at hand and to request salaries that corresponded to the size of their churches, the cost of living in their location, and the level of responsibility people were carrying.

SHORT OF THE GOAL

While the new financial structure granted some local autonomy, the constraints to apostolic immediacy and visionary breakthrough remained because of the 'fiscal glue' mentality. For example, if a church purchased a building, the mortgage was still held under the legal identity of the central trust. The seven people who held positions on the National Leadership Team were legally responsible for everything, and this limited the scope of what we could do as a movement. We could only progress as far as the National Leadership Team as a whole could see. Because the movement was still technically one legal identity, every decision—or at the very least, the ratification of every decision—was made by a handful of people who could never truly understand the complexities churches faced in each locality. We were a long way from genuinely empowering those who were down in the trenches where the battles were truly fought and won.

This led to mounting frustrations. Imagine a mum and dad who have two daughters, one who has come of age and the other who is still a child.

It makes sense that they would administer the younger one's bank account and have significant input into what she does and doesn't spend her money on. With the older daughter, however, sensible parents would challenge her to learn to thrive independently and responsibly as an adult, but ultimately, they would not control her right to administrate her own affairs. There was no other way to look at it. Our movement was holding out on its churches, treating them like infants when they needed to take responsibility and grow up.

Of course, the power of our combined leveraged equity provided a very legitimate reason to maintain the status quo. If the movement owned everything in a single entity, it was easy for the National Leadership Team to go to a bank on behalf of a church and say, "We have 100 million dollars in assets and plenty of equity, so could you lend us more for an additional building?" However, this advantage was a double-edged sword, just as it is for a rich kid who has everything handed to them. They never develop the muscle to make it in their own right.

The downside for the movement was that individual churches took very little ownership and they didn't need faith. There was no need for them to stretch and see God come through for them. For individual churches to obtain finance in their own right would have been much more difficult, or impossible in some cases; but on the other hand, having to fight for it is a pressure that draws out the congregation's generosity and activates their faith, helping rather than hindering a movement's overall position.

Philosophically, I believe that the more we empower leadership at a grassroots level, the more ownership we will achieve. In turn, this encourages widespread responsibility over the whole organisation. The more we push down the accountability and responsibility to the local church level, the better. I come from an entrepreneurial background. My parents, my brother and I all had farms. I could only imagine how I would have felt if my father had said, "Well Bruce, you can have a farm, but I'm going to look after all the money." I would have been frustrated. Thankfully, my father had a healthier view of how to launch his sons, and I was able to learn to manage every aspect of the farming challenge and become successful in my own right.

THE NUTS AND BOLTS

If we were going to free up our leaders on the ground, we needed to amend two important documents relating to the movement's trusts. The first was called the trust deed. This wasn't an overly wordy document. It simply spelt out how we legally governed our affairs, like a constitution or set of rules for operating. It included the fact that we had agreed to have no less than five trustees (and no more than a certain number as well), along with guidelines around how those trustees were to be appointed. It also included our statement of belief and our objectives. The Trust Deed stated that we were a charity with a primary objective toward religion or church activities, and it determined that we particularly uphold the value of marriage as a protection of the conservative values of our community. This was a legal document, and it was important that we abided by what it contained. If anyone ever wanted to find a discrepancy or cause legal trouble for the movement, the trust deed would have been their reference point.

The other document was the Partnership Manual. This outlined our framework for practice within the movement's churches. This document defined:

1. the configuration and role of the Council
2. the Council's role in appointing a national leader
3. the role of the National Leadership Team
4. the three areas of ordination:
   a. as a minister
   b. as a notary
   c. as a credentialled marriage celebrant
5. the role of elders and other leaders
6. our approach to governance by eldership
7. practical matters about our structure
8. how finances, assets and salaries were to be managed

Changes to the Partnership Manual were needed to facilitate apostolic immediacy on the ground, but this happened in stages. The Partnership

Manual originally said that all funding was to be centralised, including salaries and assets. This had now changed. But changing our manual wasn't all that was needed. We also had a lot of unwritten laws that shaped our behaviour. These were understandings based on precedent and what was widely understood within the movement rather than anything that was in a document. The practice of salaries being set nationally was an example of this. There was an expectation that city and country salaries were all set to the same amount. This was able to be changed without revising the partnership manual, while other reforms—like the provision that allowed our churches to set up their own local trusts—did call for updates to the partnership manual.

Regardless of whether we were changing things on paper or within our shared understanding, our leadership team first needed to make a conscious decision to change. Then the community as a whole needed to be led in that direction with care to ensure the reforms gained assent and were well accepted.

When the dust settled, the landscape was different. Central control gave way to guidance. The national office began sending out a recommended pay scale every year, and it was up to the elders of individual churches to adopt that scale or not. This made it easier to manage the differences between city and country cost-of-living expenses, and the varying demands of large and small congregations. Churches could now pay their staff appropriately and recruit in ways appropriate to their mission and vision.

CHOOSING AN IMPLEMENTATION MODEL

Many corporations operate as we did in the beginning—they have one legal identity, and everything under that is a 'branch'. In my mind, we must be careful we don't take corporate values and shoehorn them to fit our church culture. I have no desire to embrace hierarchical models for our movements or our local churches. We are part of something bigger than any local church, but this does not mean we need to be a corporation. So what are we? The closest analogy I know of is the idea of a 'partnership'. It's mutual, organic and alive. We're in *partnership* together to achieve a greater kingdom cause.

There was a time when we as a global church, including our movement, needed to lift our game. We were losing ground and had become stifled and stale in our perspective. Back then, a little corporate thinking addressed that problem and seeded some great Holy Spirit innovation and reform. Churches like Hillsong and C3 helped the wider Christian community recover. They are an example of what is possible when we become open to fresh growth pathways and strategies. But like every new ideology toward renewal, it is so easy to tip the scales too far in the opposite direction, creating its own set of problems. What they modelled was valuable, but I think even now God is saying, "You don't need to throw out your own identity. Make sure the heart of who and what you are is preserved." So sure, we need to run conferences to bind communities together, we need to bring a spirit of excellence to all we do, sometimes bigger is a little better, and we need to be relevant, but we can't let the scale we're operating at become the controlling factor. For me, the idea of partnership helps us find the right balance and perspective.

After seven years as leader of the apostolic movement in New Zealand, we had gained some ground in terms of scale, but the biggest win was that a cultural shift had begun. We are stewards of culture as much as anything else, and that was improving. We had dealt with many problems and some factional issues, and peace had come into those spaces. We had begun to value our own people, and we were experiencing even greater levels of positive cultural shifts as a strong band of prophetic heroes had stepped up within the movement. As I looked to the term ahead, there seemed to be a greater sense of unity and an increased level of direction and purpose. I think people were starting to realise, "Okay, I can't blame the movement any longer. I've got to start taking responsibility." We were all growing up and coming of age together. I had been sharing my vision for many years, but now the local churches were starting to get what I had been driving at all along. It was time for another substantial reform.

10

Remaining Relevant

Imagine coming across a citrus tree in the corner of a garden that hasn't been given attention for some time. It looks neglected and is definitely not thriving. You stand there pondering all the effort required to make it fruitful again. You decide to begin by giving it a good pruning. You clear the weeds around the base of the tree and give it a good drenching—only to discover once the sun has fully risen that the tree is still completely shaded. Realising that a towering tree nearby is obscuring your citrus tree from the light, you wake up the next morning and get to work. Finding a more suitable position, you dig up the tree and move it there, then you water your citrus tree once again. Finally, you add some fertiliser to facilitate fresh growth. You walk away confident that your tree will soon have a whole new lease on life.

AN IMAGE PROBLEM

In the same way, our work of reforming the movement was multifaceted and involved many more changes than we first anticipated. One of these involved our name. We were still called the *Apostolic Churches of New Zealand*, but the name wasn't doing us any favours among the community at large. We needed to drop the word 'apostolic' to stay relevant. The word was not widely understood, and it had become somewhat stale in its use. Of course, the old name perfectly communicated our heartbeat and

DNA—the apostolic and five-fold giftings were so important in terms of our identity and purpose—but we needed to remove what had become a stumbling block for emerging generations.

In the New Zealand context, the word 'apostolic' carried a negative connotation and caused a less-than-positive reaction. To put it bluntly, with that in our name we were perceived as a bit cultish. One of the reasons for this was that there happened to be an actual cult in New Zealand called the 'New Apostolic Church', and that somewhat tainted us and our name. There was another group who also used the name 'apostolic'. They were very closed off and had some wildly mixed-up doctrines and views. From an outreach point of view, being associated with either of those groups, even in name, was far from helpful.

Within the body of Christ in New Zealand, we had good favour and were respected. We were not seen as radical or extreme. We were recognised as a good, strong Pentecostal movement. Nevertheless, we were unnecessarily disadvantaged by the word, 'apostolic', so to be true to our kingdom vision, we needed to take a big step to stay relevant—we needed to change our name.

GETTING BUY-IN

It was my idea to change our name, and I proposed what the new name could be—but ultimately, God was prompting me to address this issue. One day, I was looking at the registered name of our Trust, and it got me thinking. When I saw it written down: 'Apostolic Church Trust Board', I said to myself, "Okay, we sort of have an acronym here. We could call ourselves ACTS!" I also realised that using an acronym would soften things for those who would find the change difficult, because the meaning was still there.

In preparation to bring my proposal to the National Leadership Team, I put in a lot of work and prayer beforehand. It's not my style to go into a meeting and say, "I think we need to change this or that. Does anyone have any good ideas?" Instead, I build a case in my mind. In this situation, I asked myself, "What contemporary term best represents the apostolic context? How can I make the name more relevant?" I was looking for a way to link the word 'apostolic' and the acronym ACTS when a biblical connection came to my mind. The book of Acts is called The Acts of the Apostles. This association was a bridge linking the word with the acronym! With that in mind, I got into communication mode, asking myself questions like, "How am I going to get this across? What am I going to say?" In the end, I found some useful language that I could use to bring my idea to the team: "We are writing the twenty-ninth chapter of the Book of Acts."

I'm not sure if the team just liked the name, if I was convincing, or if we all just knew it was time for this change, but the idea was well received and quickly decided upon with little discussion. Next, I brought it to the Council, and again, it was well received. Then I said, "If we are going to adopt this name, we need to take it on tour."

Generally, we got an amazing buy-in by approaching it the way we did. After making the decision, we travelled to every centre within the country as part of the annual National Leadership Tour, gathering as many people as we could to communicate the change. We focused on our young people understanding and owning what we were proposing. In many ways, this change was about them and their ongoing effectiveness as the future heirs of the movement, and their response was enthusiastic. In the entire week of the tour, we received only one objection. This was from an older person who stood up and said, "If we do this, we're touching history. Why do we have to change our name? It is who we are." It was a fair enough comment. But immediately, a younger person stood up and said, "Well, you don't understand. The word 'apostolic' does not help us in our relationships and connection with our friends. If we can say we're part of ACTS, that is a name that we can carry, and one we can hold onto."

I'm sure there were plenty of older people who were also reluctant, but the moment our young people started to articulate the value of this for them, those who were yet to be fully convinced did a truly honourable thing and gave way to the emerging generation. They could see that this change was worth the cost.

The acceptance of the name ACTS on the National Leadership Tour was strong. From there, all we had to do was update our legal documents to reflect the change.

It was only after we had changed our name that I remembered a word given by a recognised prophet years prior: "There will come a time when this movement will walk with a new name." This was at a Council meeting I attended at El Rancho in Waikanae in the 1990s, well before I became national leader. I guess that word was always at the back of my mind.

A lot of other churches and movements changed their name over the years, hoping that this would seed the changes in culture they knew they needed, but we did things the other way around and I think it was the only real option. We changed our culture first. We'd made massive organisational shifts, and now our name was catching up. It was like the icing on the cake, a signal to us of what we had accomplished together.

A SUCCESS STORY

Changing our name to ACTS put an end to many other problems by default. A whole lot of issues just went away at that point. Just as a new set of clothes can subconsciously help the way you carry yourself, we were rejuvenated and fresh life was flowing in our veins. I look back and I am still amazed at how quickly the new name was adopted. It was as though we were all prepared. The way our people rallied behind the new name was an expression of the energy they already possessed.

Everything, including our annual conference, had its branding changed immediately to reflect the new name. People everywhere picked it up and ran with it. It was timely. We were ready, and God's favour was all over it. It demonstrates that in leadership, momentum is so powerful. I was being obedient, so I made a move in a good direction, but the strong and universal uptake of what I proposed made it successful. This was so valuable to me and my leadership. If you're trying to change something and you don't have buy-in from the outset, you'll be in for a struggle—but if it goes well, people won't question it. You won't have to fight to justify your actions because momentum speaks for itself. This was an important high point in my journey as the national leader because the momentum we had developed was such a contrast to what things were like when I first accepted the role.

People started to ask enthusiastically if they should rename their churches. Should they include the name of the movement, and swap out the word 'apostolic' for 'ACTS'? I was hesitant to let that happen because I felt ACTS should be a name that identified our partnership together as a movement rather than individual local churches. In response, we said they could use it alongside their church's name, indicating that it was part of ACTS Churches New Zealand. We agreed that their names and their sense of identity should be shaped by the communities they represented and the vision they carried and that ACTS was an umbrella for their wider relational networks, as well as a credentialling body for the movement. As such, no one would be ordained as an Equippers pastor or any other network minister. We were all ACTS pastors.

Over time we also renamed our 'Council of Apostles' to a 'Council of Ascension Ministry Gifts'. This brought alignment to our vision while widening the scope of who could serve and lead on the council. It signalled that we were now free to bring people forward on the basis of their gifting, even if they were not apostles. Now, we could ask, "Who are the mature people? Whose voices should be heard? Women, men, teachers, prophets . . . who should be on the council?" This change was especially significant because it made way for a wider array of young voices to rise and take their place.

The success of what we had accomplished gave me confidence to pursue the entirety of the vision I carried. We had made progress, but we weren't there yet. Apostolic immediacy in line with our Welsh Revival roots was still a little way off.

STRUCTURAL CHANGE

11

Changing of the Guard

My vision was threefold—we were to remove structure that hindered the execution of apostolic-led vision within our movement, we needed to stay relevant, and it was important for us to make way for the emerging generation. On the first two points we had made some progress and I felt it was time to concentrate on the third. It was time for some of the older leaders to stand aside, to make room so that younger ones could take their place.

MAKING ROOM FOR THE NEXT GENERATION

I knew we would become stale and irrelevant if we didn't bring new blood in, so I went to the council not very long after I had become the national leader and posed a question. "I'm asking some of you to consider not standing again for Council," I began. "I want to bring younger people in so they can gain a greater understanding of the leadership and operation of the movement. This is about us getting behind the next generation, backing them in their calling, and equipping them to function at another level. We need to forge something new." Some of the council members immediately agreed and stepped back willingly. With their support, we were able to begin moving in the direction of our vision.

As the national leader, I had the right to invite people to the annual council meetings, so I brought some key young leaders in who I thought would serve well in this setting. At least they were now in the room, and that went a long way toward achieving the changes we were looking for. It meant that when the time came to appoint council members, we had new people to choose from who were already present.

These younger members came and participated, but at that time they had no power to vote because they weren't on the council. Still, it was a beginning that set them up so they could be known by the others before the next election. Their presence prior to the election allowed the other council members to see the gift they carried and gauge the character of the person as well. It took some courage at first for many of the younger ones to speak up when they had something to say, but a few did. I was also being transparent and forthright about what we were trying to achieve. Of course, the council members could elect whoever they wanted during each election cycle, but generally speaking, they allowed me to lead the way and began making room for younger people to serve.

At each National Conference, we would recognise council members who were finishing their term, and we'd celebrate their contribution by publicly honouring them. If a person had been serving for a long time, we would honour them financially as well. In the first year, we made a point of bringing in a younger council, but it took us a while to significantly shift the balance from old to new. It was a progression. We were constantly saying, "We need to keep this fresh; we need to keep it young." However, now that I was getting older it became more complicated for me because I was staying behind while asking other older members to move aside. Yet even though they could see what was happening, they were more than gracious to me.

A lot of our emerging ACTS leaders were coming through the Equippers movement. This is partly because a gift on my life is the ability to spot leaders, and Equippers was set up to foster them. I've always had a sense of who could rise to a higher level of leadership, and we supported whoever we could. This caused tension at times. Not every person or church can produce leaders—many suppose they can, but that's not always true. Often, they miss what's right in front of their nose. It's relatively common for people to be so focused on what they want to happen, that they miss the potential in those around them to rise and execute the vision. As a result, very little is achieved, and the next generation is stifled.

Once the council votes to select the National Leader, the person appointed can choose their team for that year. I chose to pack my team with emerging leaders. That immediately brought them into the room and therefore to the forefront of what was happening. Bringing in useful and innovative people kept the dynamics fresh. The national leader typically also has the advantage of submitting potential candidates to the Council. Once these emerging leaders were on the National Leadership Team, they naturally progressed toward finding their voice on the Council, and that worked well for us.

Not all movements work this way. Some include all their credentialled ministers as their council. Other movements also include representatives from among their church membership. The key leaders and National Leadership Team or executive are elected from this body. We have chosen not to go down that path because we are trying to mirror nationally what we want to happen locally.

In choosing my leadership team, I was looking for people who carried some sort of 'x-factor' and who could understand and appreciate each other's differences. I have found that it is unwise as a leader to surround yourself only with 'yes-people'. At the same time, you need a team of people you can work with. That's where chemistry comes in. Bill Hybels once said, "When you're forming a team, you want character, you want gifts, and you want chemistry." It is important that we do not overlook this third dynamic among our future leaders.

KNOWING WHERE WE FIT

One of the challenges in supporting leadership development is that many people have a wrong impression of their gifting and identity. I could see we were struggling with this, even within the Council, so I decided to take the Council members through a process. "I'm going to spend some time with you on the teaching around motivation giftings in Romans twelve," I told them. "After that, I'm going to talk about the essential ministry gifts—what they are, what they look like, and how they should find expression. Then I'm going to ask you to identify on a piece of paper where you feel you fit in terms of ministry gifting." When each person had written their responses, I asked them to share their 'motivation gifting' with everyone in the room, and what they perceived their essential ministry to be. Then I said, "Okay, now we're going to go around the room again, and this time everybody else is going to tell you what they perceive your gifting to be."

That exercise changed people's lives. Most people were overestimating their giftings. I wanted to shepherd them constructively so they could see themselves with more clarity. I wanted to equip them to value their gift rightly and to step into it with confidence so they could truly take their rightful place. Many saw themselves as apostles, even though that grace was not evident in their lives. It was time to shift the perception that they had to be an apostle to oversee or lead.

This is an important perspective. You don't have to be an apostle to be a leader! Pastors can look after leaders. They have a grace to speak into the lives and even marriages of those they lead. The same principle applies to teachers and prophets and evangelists. On the Council we had great pastors, teachers and prophets, and we needed them to function confidently and well in those gifts. We needed to recognise that not everyone has the apostolic authority to come in and take the group to a whole other place, or to oversee a significant shift.

As leaders, we will never feel adequate, satisfied or happy when we are striving to be something we're not. Neither can we give our best contribution when we've pegged ourselves incorrectly. The process we went through that day shifted the outlook of everyone on the Council, and it changed the direction of people's lives. When we went around the room, one person identified himself as an apostle/pastor. We said to him, "We don't see you as an apostle, we see you as a pastor/evangelist. Maybe that is why you are frustrated and why your people are frustrated too."

Steve Graham is a great example of this as someone who had unsuccessfully tried to start a number of apostolic initiatives. By the end of the day, he was confident in his gifting. He left that afternoon saying, "Okay, now I understand that I'm a teacher." When Steve pursued his teaching gift, he began to flourish. He also began to contribute significantly within the movement. Once we had recognised his natural gifting, it was easy for me to say, "Well, this is where you can serve our movement. You can come in as a teacher." And he did. We brought Steve onto our National Leadership Team, and he has been amazing at listening to the prophetic voices in the room and turning them into a teaching format that has been understood and accepted by the whole group. In bringing Steve's gift to the forefront, we were able to model that you could have a national scale of ministry without being an apostle. Since then, Steve has often remarked, "Now I can look good in an environment I can't create."

That council meeting was also a significant pivot point in that it enabled us to more easily promote people to the group knowing they weren't going to be a square peg in a round hole. In bringing people forward, I could easily speak to why we would want one person or another on the national leadership team, and how they would be able to contribute. It's not a 'Council of Apostles' anymore. It's a council of *complementary ascension gifts*.

A SNOWBALLING EFFECT

People shine when they know who they are, and great momentum comes when people are successful, appreciated, and thriving. As our leaders modelled the significance of each of the gifts in all their diversity, others saw more clearly who they too could become.

When you profile all the gifts at a leadership level, it immediately becomes a point of reproduction. It is contagious. People begin to say, "Oh wow! I'm a teacher. I could be like that." The same is true for all the giftings. This is why teaching people about the ascension gifts is vitally important. Through our ministry schools, a considerable number of people are recognising their ascension gifts and being released within our movement. We identify what people are carrying, then we elevate them, we highlight them, we validate their gift, and through that process we uncover and replicate the same gift in the lives of others in a way that snowballs for us, creating a very fruitful and empowering dynamic.

Understanding our natural motivations (Romans 12) and the essential ministry gifts (Ephesians 4:11-13) is about the functioning of the diversity within the body of Christ. For instance, every time we lift up a woman in her gifting, it's an opportunity for a young woman in the audience to realise, "Wow, I can flourish here." This is how the church is strengthened. As one person is recognised and empowered, others with the same gift profile are, also empowered. They can look on and say, "If that is true of them, then it could be true of me. I can find expression in this movement." We're constructing pathways for people. We're connecting the dots for them. When we recognise each individual's gifting, we are vision-casting, because example brings clarity to belief.

SHAPED FROM DIFFERENT DIRECTIONS

When Helen and I left for London prior to my appointment as national leader, we handed the leadership of the Auckland church to our son, Sam. As his father, I naturally wanted to help him, and over the years I have, to some degree. But Sam and I are different. We're different in the way we approach things, different in our expression, and different in our giftings, but we recognise we have something to offer each other. Sam intuitively understands some things I don't, yet he is able to look to me for other things. Some of my thinking in the area of leadership development and governance has shaped him, but Sam has an edge I could never have, and that comes through in the level of expertise he operates in.

Today, Sam is the visionary leader of the global Equippers Church movement as well as the ACTS movement. He is also the one who first caught the vision for our Equippers conference (now called SHOUT Conference). I could never have run SHOUT like he has. He didn't learn to do that from me—he got that from rubbing shoulders with Russell Evans, the founder of Planetshakers. Russell came along and helped Sam take hold of something that I could never offer.

This is a key leadership dynamic: We need to be mentored by more than one person if we are to grow in all the different aspects of our leadership. An emerging leader needs a group of people they can look to as examples and as sources of inspiration and instruction. Mark is a clear biblical example of this. John Mark was initially influenced by Paul, but there came a time when they went their separate ways. Later, they picked up their relationship again, but in the meantime, Barnabas came alongside him with encouragement and had a powerful impact on Mark's life. Mark was not one of Jesus' original disciples, and it appears he leaned heavily on Peter as an eyewitness source when he wrote his Gospel. Barnabas was the mentor close at hand, while both Peter and Paul likely shaped Mark more from a distance. With this rich diversity of influence, Mark's contribution became more significant, and it remains impactful to this day.

Another key is that we must disciple people to Christ, not to ourselves, nor to any individual. In 1 Corinthians 11:1 where Paul said, "Imitate me as I imitate Christ," he wasn't thinking of numerous little 'Pauls' running around. Instead, he was encouraging people to interact with Christ as he did, so that they too could find their unique purpose and calling. This is a general principle for leaders—people don't need to be gifted or wired like us to thrive and grow under our leadership. We lose our way when we think mentoring alone is the answer, because we ultimately want to connect people to Christ rather than ourselves. That should be the only point of dependence we seek to create. If we can think and function that way, our impact will be powerful and lasting, and those coming along after us will be able to grow beyond us. This means that we can gain from the lives of others without needing to have a direct or close relationship with them. Because we are all connected to Christ, we can benefit from others even from a distance. This is true for me. Some of those who have most greatly inspired me and influenced my life are people I have never sat or even talked with.

LIFTERS, SHIFTERS AND CARRIERS

As leaders, it is helpful to differentiate between those who tend to be 'do-ers' and those who share your vision. We discover this when we move from delegation to empowerment. This requires a high level of trust. Leaders delegate when they are training people, when they're discipling them. They give someone a job and say, "This is what I want you to do," and the task has an endpoint. When the leader realises the person has what it takes, they might give them another task. But when we empower someone, we don't tell them they have to start at 8 a.m. and finish at 5 p.m. We're not looking at how much time they spend working. We start with delegation, but quickly we move to empowerment, and at that point, the focus is on outcomes (or, 'fruit'). We build the relationship and the discipline of working, and as we empower people we also increase responsibility and accountability, but then we take a step back. In their role as overseers, a lot of leaders never move from delegation to empowerment. As a result, their people never progress to the point where they can truly take the weight from them. This limits a leader's ultimate capacity in terms of the mission.

In essence, the people we lead fall into three groups: the lifters, the shifters, and the carriers. We might inspire a 'lifter' with vision, but when they look at the task required, they conclude, "Nah, that's not for me," and they put it down. A 'shifter' might look at the task and say, "Okay, I can do that." They pick it up, shift it along a little, and then put it down. In their mind, the job is done. They might say, "I'm finished, I've completed the task, I'm going home, and I don't want to be disturbed." These are the people who tend to remain in the delegation phase of leadership development.

The 'carriers' are those who own the vision. As their ownership increases, we can move their responsibility from delegation to empowerment. Now they can lead themselves. They know how to carry a task or a vision, but they also know how to take a day off. They look after themselves because they realise the pressure of ministry will always be demanding and consuming. And in the end, they are fruitful and make a difference that enables the vision.

12

New Legal Requirements

My vision for the movement had three components. After thirteen years as national leader, we had made significant progress in two of these: normalising 'kingdom' culture; and raising emerging leaders who shared both the workload and the vision. Real breakthrough in terms of local autonomy—the third component of my vision—was more difficult to achieve. Among the council, we still lacked strong consensus that this was a positive step for the movement.

However, in 2013, the New Zealand Government passed legislation that dramatically impacted more complex charitable trusts like our own. Essentially, it required a change to how we related to the government. In terms of our financial reporting and legal perspectives, we now only had two choices: to consolidate all our churches and ministries into one entity or to divide into autonomous local entities that would report to the government independently. Suddenly, the Council was faced with a decision that would be crucial to the future of our movement.

A CHALLENGE AND AN OPPORTUNITY

The more I thought about the decision we had to make, the more convinced I became that this was a God-given opportunity. It crystallised my thinking from previous years. I knew the future for us lay in becoming a bottom-up movement rather than a top-down one. Now, the government was forcing us to choose between the two. There was no way for us to stay on the fence, and this challenge held an alluring possibility: It might just propel us to become a truly grassroots movement in a quarter of the time it would have taken if our hand hadn't been forced.

The change was to come into effect in 2016, so we had only two years to decide and align ourselves one way or the other. We needed to either take a great leap forward immediately or lose a lot of hard-won ground toward local autonomy. For me, it was hardly a choice at all. In essence, the government's changes merely accelerated a trajectory we were already on.

Until now, we had operated as a single legal entity for the most part, but the government had allowed all the churches to run their own affairs. A large church, like the Auckland Equippers Church, generated a higher income than many of the others. This put it over a certain threshold, so its level of accountability was higher. Each year it would require a thorough audit. Many of the smaller churches, because their income was significantly less, didn't require auditing at all.

Under the new legislation, if there was any link of authority between different entities (such as the veto power currently held by the movement trust over local church trusts), they would be treated as a single entity. This meant that their combined, rather than individual, incomes would be evaluated against the threshold to determine the level of reporting and audit required. The entire organisation, including all of the smaller churches, would be well over the threshold, and would all be included in the annual audit. This would have been immediately crippling on an administrative level. If we did not act to break the organisation into individual charitable trusts, we would need to consolidate all of our bank accounts and associated accounting, centralising them so they would be owned and managed by the movement.

In essence, we would either have to genuinely operate as a single unit with rigorous controls and unsustainable administrative overheads, or we had to divide, and somehow empower each unit to thrive and be accountable to the government in its own right. Neither option was easy, but the writing was on the wall.

I needed to be prepared, and we as a council needed to get ahead of this challenge. Any way we sliced it, this was going to be a mountain of work, and I knew we would require significant help on the financial front. I asked Desiree Levy to come along to the council meeting, where we were talking about transition options in light of the new legislation. Desiree and her husband Will were Equippers pastors, and she was a Chartered Accountant, someone whose judgement I trusted. I wanted Desiree to hear the conversation so I could ask her opinion about the situation afterwards. At that time, we had no one managing our finances internally. Ever since David Kent, our accountant of many years, had passed away, we had contracted out the work that he had historically done for us in-house. Desiree was able to conduct some research for us and provide advice to the council in the lead-up to the annual meeting so we could be as prepared as possible.

MAKING THE DECISION

At the next council meeting, the conversation came down to whether we should consolidate or make our churches completely autonomous. The second option would involve shifting real estate into each church's possession, and on this recommendation, one of the council members held out as a lone voice. He said, "Well, we can still hold all the buildings in a separate entity and let the churches have administrative autonomy without shifting the large assets."

The general feeling, however, moved in the other direction, to the point where the majority were thinking, "We're going to do this. Let's do it, and if we are going to do it, let's do it properly." The general consensus was that we had been on a journey, and now it was time to take the final step. That trend in the conversation disturbed the only opposing voice greatly. I guess he couldn't imagine the movement holding together under a more organic model with the assets distributed. I think every one of us valued what had been created over the years, as he did, and we all wanted the best for the future, but it was difficult for him to consent to this change, and he left the meeting.

Eventually, we decided to break the organisation into autonomous units.

It was already 2015, so we only had one year to implement this historic change. It was also an election year for the council, so I had to resubmit my vision to continue in the national leader role. I asked the council for another two years to complete this work knowing there would be a lot of moving parts to roll out, and thankfully the council agreed to grant me that.

THE HELP WE NEEDED

The moment we ratified our course of action officially, I sought legal assistance, because this was a huge job and it would need to be managed with as much help as possible. We found a suitable candidate in Warwick Cambridge from Preston Russell Law, a lawyer who was a Christian and understood charities. He was my age, or maybe slightly older, and quite involved with the Presbyterian churches. At first, he assumed that we would want to continue as a single entity and he persisted in telling us what we had to do so that this could be accomplished, but it was not what we wanted and it was not what we had decided as a council, so we needed to keep pushing back. I'd say, "No, that's not the way we want to go. We are not trying to maintain a hierarchical structure. We want to go in the other direction." I guess the lawyer was trying to interpret it through his Presbyterian framework. In the end, he caught on to what we were doing and became a significant support on the legal side for the entire project.

I asked Desiree if she would consider leading the change process. Desiree and Will had been with us in London and were engaged with us in the leadership and life of the church there. After we came back to New Zealand, we called them to pastor Equippers in Masterton. At that time, Desiree was also working as a practising accountant. When the legislation changed, Will and Desiree had been back in New Zealand for about five years, and they now had a young family.

We agreed together as a council that Desiree would do the work on a project basis for the next couple of years and that we would keep this separate from the movement's business-as-usual activities. Desiree understood what the project involved. She already had many years of experience working with charitable trusts and audits. She was familiar with the stream of amendments to business and trust law that had come across her desk as part of her regular job. Having been part of an inter-church accountancy working group that included Anglicans, Catholics and many other church groups, she also had a wonderful collection of useful contacts. Thankfully, Desiree didn't need a lot of convincing to take on this huge task and was able to get started and get runs on the board much more quickly than I expected. She was a gift from God for the movement, as far as I was concerned.

THE PROJECT GOES FORWARD

Desiree understood Charities Service's expectations. She was able to work with lawyers on our behalf and negotiate with the banks. Working with the banks was essential because all our buildings and mortgages needed to be shifted away from the central body and into local entities. That took some thought—and careful analysis. Each building required us to compare the amount of equity with the loan amounts required, and it was our job to convince the banks that appropriate security was held for each new loan that we were establishing. For some, the maths worked fine, and in other situations, we faced the downside of no longer having centralised property holdings—churches in weaker financial positions could no longer borrow from a combined pool of equity or leverage the equity held by those who owned their buildings freehold.

We had sixty churches in the movement, but there were about ninety entities in total because some churches had also set up social enterprises or community service trusts. We needed to ensure that all of these were legally changed into local autonomous charitable trusts as well. It all represented an unbelievably large pile of paperwork. It was Desiree's job to establish local church trusts in every location. She contracted a capable person to help with the task. This man worked alongside her full-time, looking after all the data, the numbers, the people, and the forms. His job was to ensure that every piece of paper got signed and filed away properly.

As each entity was formed, complete with its new assets, we needed to train local people to fulfil their new roles and responsibilities. Because accountability was now held at the grassroots level, these people needed to know what they were doing. Otherwise, this was never going to work. There were a lot of people to manage. Each of the ninety entities had five trustees, meaning four hundred and fifty people needed to have a very clear idea of how charitable trusts operate. Both the ones giving the training and everyone receiving it did admirably. It was a huge learning curve for everyone.

From the time the legislation was passed, we had two years to become fully compliant. Desiree was aware of the cut-off date and worked tirelessly to complete this challenge and meet every legal requirement. A small thing like changing a bank account came with a lot of downstream work at the local level—like donations and rebates. Desiree had to ensure that everything was carefully passed across to the new entities, so good communication was necessary to let everyone know what was going on. Until then, we had also managed all the pastor's salaries and their leave entitlements centrally. Pushing this out locally and getting people on the ground conversant with the complexities of human resourcing matters was another phenomenal undertaking.

At the local level, there was no problem with a church or entity receiving the property onto their books. Some accounting entries had to happen for that. But once the transfer was complete, the local church had to learn how to record the depreciation of such a large asset and manage all the other associated matters that were formerly handled by the head office. Now local church budgets took on more significance because the local leadership not only had to know their numbers, they needed to know what the end of the financial year was now going to look like and what would be required in their reporting. There was also a new sense of needing to be sustainable and profitable at the local level, a requirement for the local leadership that had never been there before.

As all this was happening, I was working with the National Leadership Team. We were having conversations with pastors and other church leaders, making sure every change was getting the endorsement and support needed.

So many people had to do so much work, and on the whole, our people were legendary. This was true across the nation. A great number of people contributed—from the lawyers to the auditors and the tax accountants on speed dial, to the people at Charities Services who were trying to help all the charities that were impacted by the new legislative changes. The overall challenge was to ensure that before two years were up, we were operating in a way where our practice matched our new legal form. The good thing about all the pressure was that we had a ticking clock obliging us to transform the movement quickly into what we had ultimately wanted to become. And then suddenly, it was all over. It was done, and we'd met the deadline.

We breathed a collective sigh of relief, but we couldn't stop for long. We wanted our pastors to be empowered in their local settings to make the best decisions they could, and to have the information necessary to accomplish that. This meant they needed to be able to read and understand their reports, and to know what the numbers meant. We also needed to create structures to support the local churches so they could stay on top of governance, financial and legal matters, health and safety, and child protection policies. Desiree continued to contribute, building teams to help with this. Margaret Hollingsworth, who had previously looked after wages, invoicing and on-charging, had helped with the project and was now able to join the others in training the churches, answering their queries and providing support. We were all aware there was a long tail to this very intense project.

13

Structure that Works

Dividing our movement into ninety separate 'pieces' was a huge accomplishment, but for every piece to be recognised by Charities Services, we needed to ensure that nothing was binding any of them to the previous hierarchical system, where one trust was obligated to another. The movement itself was part of a trust, but its relationship to the other eighty-nine trusts had to be loose enough that in no sense was it controlling. This came down to the way they were structured legally.

ENSURING INDEPENDENCE

The project through which we had reinvented ourselves had completely changed every legal document we possessed. By the time it was over, nothing pertaining to our organisational structure from the previous season was left in the filing cabinet. Changing all the legal structures meant that our partnership manual now also needed to be updated to harmonise with the new system. Charities Services worked through all our documentation, checking everything meticulously to ensure that we were genuinely setting up autonomous churches and that there wasn't a hidden link obliging the new trusts to submit to the central trust. It was all about getting the paperwork right, and ensuring the documents for the new church trusts represented each church's reality. From a legal perspective, we only had the goodwill of our people, our partnership manual, and the structures defined in those documents, to hold us together as a movement.

Warwick Cambridge led the way through the legalities, and his son James did a lot of the legwork for us. He was a lawyer too. Someone at that time had left the movement a significant monetary gift in their will, and that covered all the legal costs. This was phenomenal because it meant that we didn't need to find the money.

I did much of the work drafting changes to the partnership manual. There was quite a bit there from the previous version that was directly transferrable, and after our discussions with Warwick, I had a fair idea of what was necessary and required. When I was finished, he reviewed it. We designed a template for the structure of each church trust and then reused it over and over. Once we had got it working in the first few instances, it was less effort to get subsequent trusts created and approved because we had clarified our thinking with Charities Services in the earlier cases.

KEEPING IN STEP AS A MOVEMENT

As part of the templated structure, each trust had five board members. This included the senior minister and the overseer of the church, both credentialled representatives of the movement. The other three board positions were occupied by church members. This meant that two of the five members of each board had an obligation to represent and consider the interests of the movement as a whole, as well as the individual church's interests. Importantly, they were not a majority so there was no sense of the movement having any control or power over the church's boards through this mechanism. This gave ACTS some influence among the churches, but it prevented the movement from having the level of power Charities Services would have expected from a singular entity rather than a distributed network of like-minded trusts.

From then on, the ongoing representation of ACTS depended on the management of leadership credentials, a job which the National Leadership team took seriously as we moved forward. Ideally, reputable people are appointed who continue to carry the movement's vision passionately and demonstrate great character—and everything flows easily from that premise. It's a rare event that would cause someone's suitability to continue to hold their ACTS credential to come into question, and even less likely that we would revoke a credential, but the clause is there if needed. For instance, a disclosure of moral failure on the part of a senior minister would involve their credential being revoked. That would essentially force them to resign because without the credential they are not eligible to hold that office or to occupy the place of the senior leader on the board. At best, the board could appoint them to one of the three non-credentialled places. In any case, without the senior leader role occupied, that trust would cease to function legally. ACTS would need to appoint a new credentialled senior leader so that things could function properly again.

It is much the same for the overseeing minister. In the movement, we have a pool of credentialled overseeing ministers, and any of them can be approached by a senior pastor who is seeking an overseer. Usually, these appointments are relationally based. In many cases, the overseer may not even live geographically close to the local church but is able to attend board meetings remotely. Either way, he or she is credentialled by the movement, and a trust cannot operate without that person in place. The overseeing minister becomes the representative of the National Leadership Team on that trust and an important communication link between the two, ensuring the local church trust and the movement are in step with one another. Most of the time, this role functions positively, enhancing the experience of being part of the movement for the local church and its board by ensuring that it gets the needed support.

A SUPERIOR TYPE OF GLUE

The credentials held by the senior minister and overseer function as a sort of 'canary in the mine'—a safety gauge for all concerned. This indicates whether or not everything is working well. ACTS has no financial interest to preserve in being a credentialling body, nor is there any sense of domination over local board decisions. Instead, the aim is for all of the individual churches and trusts to travel together, carrying the same culture, knowing their collective identity, and displaying similar distinctive traits.

Our credential communicates that the candidate is in a healthy place in their soul, their mind and their heart. It verifies that this person understands the significance of the movement and is mature and equipped enough to lead and represent it well. These appointed senior ministers and overseers care about the movement as a whole, and it seems reasonable to place the relationship between the movement's central body and an individual church in their hands.

I had always been very uncomfortable with the statement, "The central ownership of buildings is the fiscal glue that holds our movement together," but our new structure, together with our ACTS credentials, had now become a different kind of adhesive, gently and organically holding us together. Character, culture and a sense of shared identity and purpose were now there, helping us to link hands and walk together as a community.

Of course, if the Holy Spirit wasn't leading, we would have lost our way, but in the end, our pursuit was rewarded with the sense that we had arrived at a solution that was both practical and attractive, especially since we had no desire to create dependence in the periphery. Instead, the whole project of reinventing ourselves became about grassroots empowerment, wraparound training, and supporting each trust to ensure it had what it needed to succeed in its own right.

GRASSROOTS EMPOWERMENT

It takes more than formal structures to define and shape church life. Each of our churches has a group of elders as well as a board, and while there is often some overlap, the elders also have a spiritual role which doesn't interfere with the senior pastor's ability to make decisions. One person on their own can't make something happen—they have to work with others so that the entire church is united and engaged. Together, the senior pastor, board of trustees, and elders can help build ownership on the ground. This is important because if the community is on a specific faith journey—for instance, the acquisition of a new building—a broad buy-in will be essential.

The elders also have a care role toward the senior pastor. This was always important, but under the new structure, as a little more responsibility fell on the senior pastor—to generate wages, run a profitable and sustainable operation, and manage health and safety requirements—their care was more valuable than ever.

Some things became more complex for the central leadership too. Previously, if we as the movement leadership thought a senior minister's time was coming to an end, we could act on that with very little consultation. Now we needed to engage with the individual board and the eldership of that particular church. Even so, the shift of responsibility was incredibly positive for our movement. It felt much like watching a teenage son or daughter come of age. On one hand, it was a bittersweet moment as we released the churches, but we also realised we were witnessing them navigating and leading well in life and ministry in their own right, and we understood this was exactly the way things were meant to be. We couldn't help but feel incredibly proud of the shift and development that had eventuated.

Our local leaders carry great responsibility now, and they have risen to the challenge. The senior leader of each church needs to lead their elders as well or they won't be able to function properly in their role. There are also four other people on the board; the local leader isn't a one-man or one-woman majority. Nevertheless, the senior leader needs to lead their whole community and be very adept at communicating their God-given vision. They need to cultivate unity by investing relationally because no one at any level or in any role is in a position to force others to comply. Perhaps the leader will need to share more deeply, listen more intently, or pray more frequently. True leadership always demands a certain level of energy and engagement, and taking shortcuts to run roughshod over what is in the hearts and minds of those around us is out of step with the culture of the kingdom we all represent.

Even so, the responsibility lies within the leadership. In one instance, a leader had made a mistake, signing some donation receipts that were out of step with their official donee status. When Charities Services uncovered these issues in an audit, the responsibility landed at a local level and could have easily resulted in the church being deregistered. The local church was held accountable; however, rather than being detrimental, this was a good thing. The church worked closely with our support team and the Inland Revenue Department to resolve the problem. This experience helped all the leaders to understand the seriousness of their tasks and their need to conform responsibly to the required regulations.

With all these changes in place and so many other responsibilities becoming localised, Sam and the leadership team continue to work closely with emerging and experienced leaders, holding regular governance training days to support teams as they grow into their responsibilities. We are not seeing other organisations invest at the same level in local leadership readiness, but we are convinced that everything we can do in this regard will pay dividends. The resilience and creativity we are seeing formed in our leaders under this pressure, and with our support, raises hope that we are changing the game in terms of carrying out the vision for generations to come.

WIDER APPLICATION OF OUR MODEL

The New Zealand government's current legislative position for charitable trusts applies to a limited context, but we see our learnings and approach as highly transferable to many other church movements. For instance, Equippers uses aspects of this model when it operates internationally, working with a national credentialing body there to replicate the structure we use here in New Zealand as much as possible among our churches in that particular country. What we have is a scalable and cohesive model of local empowerment that others can adopt and take advantage of.

Along the way, many people put in a lot of effort to solve some challenging problems, and with all of that said and done, it is natural to take a step back and look at where we have arrived. In so doing, I realise that God has achieved something in and through us all that is more significant than we ever foresaw. I see that we have been gifted a model that values leaders at the local level and places trust in them in ways that hierarchical leadership never can because it has no reason to. We set out to unfetter apostolic leadership on the ground, and in so doing we have achieved far more. In freeing local autonomy, we have released senior ministers and overseeing ministers to grow in their own leadership through their particular pressures and constraints, a sort of 'innovate-or-perish' scenario because they are no longer protected by the weight of a centralised movement. This encourages our intimacy with God as we take prayer to a new level, finding inspirational and creative answers that drive us forward as a movement. The quality and capacity of our leaders and the refining of the gifts they carry as they are forged in the fire of increased responsibility positions us well for the future. We see these dynamics, too, as being directly transferable to other movements all over the world.

This brings me to a final thought on the subject of structure that works. Trust is the all-important key. Hierarchy doesn't trust—it demands. What we have become is, in my opinion, something healthier, something that God can work with that can bless and prosper many, something that we as a wider community can own with a sense of joy. Things are better now for us, and perhaps there is something in our journey that others can borrow so they can share that sense for their movement or organisation.

Trust is wonderful but difficult. You have to find the right people, however, with the right foundation, trust becomes a self-fulfilling prophecy. It changes people, even when it is given before it is truly deserved. It is a tangible way of saying to people that we are going on a journey with them. We are investing in leadership for a lifetime, and if there are a few bumps along the way, that is a small thing compared to what we might be able to accomplish together under God, especially when we think of decades of service and influence. Not only that, leaders formed in a context of trust will trust others in turn, enabling the works of our hands to multiply and prosper until we contribute to a generational legacy.

When we formed a structure that assumed trust in our leaders, this was an example and an impartation from us to them. We came into the room with a strong sense of where we wanted things to go, but it was essential that we remain open as well. As leaders we need to hear the others in the room, to benefit from their gifts. Leadership is about being trusted—*and* trusting others! We need to pay attention when vital prophetic input is released or wisdom from someone else's experience is expressed. That's what makes leadership exciting—it revolves around no single person.

I often say, "I can bake the cake well, but I'm terrible at putting the icing on it." In other words, I might contribute eighty percent of the vision, but I want others to contribute the other twenty, especially when it allows them the joy of being on the cutting edge of its execution. No one wants to sit in your meeting if you are only using it to rubber stamp your ideas. Trust opens us up to the powerful clarity that others carry. It breeds good culture and builds momentum. It expands our capacity and safeguards the longevity and breadth of our influence. It is an expansive force that multiplies our leadership potential. As a movement, we have arrived at a structure that is bathed in trust. It is our hope that our example and journey will benefit many beyond our movement as well.

14

Closing Loopholes

The ideals we had fixed our eyes on were pleasing, and the work we had done to pursue that vision had landed us so close to what we had intended; however, to bed these substantial changes into our movement we needed to refine the model slightly and add in safeguards to account for the actions of some whose aspirations were not aligned to ours.

As a community, we had reached to embody kingdom values, but we had also left ourselves somewhat vulnerable. This became an issue twice when a few remaining loopholes allowed us to be taken advantage of. Thankfully, God saw our hearts and miraculously intervened in both cases so that we had time to apply mitigations without suffering any consequences.

In retrospect, how we fixed what we had built turned out to be as significant as the construction itself. How we relationally dealt with these challenges was key as well. During one of these challenges, the seeds of institutionalism could have been sown once more. In response, we maintained the spirit of the work, but we dotted the i's and crossed the t's so that what we had put in place would continue to have value for generations to come.

PALMERSTON NORTH STEALTHILY WITHDRAWS

Each senior minister requires a great deal of local focus, but the overseer of a local church needs to be conscious of the national whole, thoughtfully protecting its interests. If there's trouble brewing, the overseer's job is to keep the national leadership fully informed and to represent the interests of the movement as the situation unfolds. This was highlighted when our Palmerston North church, which had already been struggling with the movement generally, took advantage of the new structure, and when they discovered a loophole in what had been set up, the leadership of this church decided to use it to separate from the movement—and to take the church building with them.

Unfortunately, the person who occupied the overseer position on the Palmerston North church board supported this move, and in doing so, worked against the unspoken trust we had established as a dominant building block whilst tidying up our new legal structures. This slender thread of trust weaving the movement and the overseers representing local church trusts together, wasn't sufficient to push a dysfunctional situation into an intended 'timeout' where issues could be disclosed and discussed.

This showed us that one safeguard was missing. Our partnership manual stated that we were 'reliant on the goodwill of the local church board to communicate legal changes'. Palmerston North had made legal changes which we had no knowledge of, and their overseer had not updated the National Leadership Team about what was happening on the local level. The church board had gone behind our back, and we were completely in the dark about it because the overseer had simply not followed guidelines and fulfilled obligations that were clearly understood—but not written in the Partnership Manual. This meant that we were not able to discuss and work with the church on what they wanted to do. It was a breach of 'goodwill', an unethical action rather than an illegal one. Even so, we quickly realised that we needed to tighten the wording in the partnership manual.

To all intents and purposes, we had followed the lead of the Holy Spirit in revolutionising the way our movement was constituted, pushing through opposition from voices who doubted that the degree we were trusting our people would work for us. Perhaps this situation—and one other that eventuated—justified their fears, but in both cases the movement experienced miraculous interventions that saved great fallout.

After this issue came to light and we discovered the loophole, we determined to add a needed safeguard to the partnership manual at the very next council meeting. In the meantime, the Holy Spirit was gracious to help us pick up the slack. He ensured that what was hidden was brought to light and that secrets which rendered our movement vulnerable were revealed.

The change to the partnership manual was small but significant. It stated that overseers were obliged to consult with the National Leadership Team on any proposed legal changes to their church trusts ahead of time. It was no longer optional or a matter of goodwill. If the situation ever arose again, the overseer would be legally obliged to tell the National Leadership Team, who would then come alongside and find a resolution together with the local church. In the worst-case scenario, we could pause the operation of the local trust until the movement and the local leadership appointed mutually agreeable candidates to facilitate the overseer and/or the senior minister roles on the board. The wording we added to our partnership manual operated as a safeguard that ensured both local and national interests were represented well going forward.

Before the situation in Palmerston North came to light, the overseer had partnered with the senior minister's approach of not considering the movement in their proposed plans, figuring they were autonomous now. I see what unfolded next as miraculous. We received a letter from the senior minister stating that their church wanted to leave the movement but confessing they hadn't gone about it the right way. They now wanted to change that!

We began to work with the church leadership, bringing understanding that there was historical value in the real estate that needed to be considered—that the equity in the Palmerston North building had been built significantly over the years through the generosity and sacrifice of multiple generations and that it was far from integral for a senior minister who had only been leading that church for a few years to withdraw the value of that asset from the use of the movement. Unfortunately, the overseer had already signed a document empowering the leader to do just that, and it was legally binding.

I wrote back to the pastor saying we were happy for the church to leave the movement but requested they slow the process down and work through the issues properly and honourably. God miraculously moved in the heart of the senior leader causing him to reach out, with the result that all loose ends were tied and the departure ended well. In the end, they left the movement, but we retained the old building.

After that, if a church chose to leave the movement, the onus was on both parties to consider the historical value of the buildings and real estate.

CHRISTCHURCH TAKES ADVANTAGE

During the period between when we began operating with our new movement structure and when we updated the partnership agreement so that overseers were obliged to communicate legal changes to their trusts, another church exploited the loophole. The common denominator in this case was that the overseer was the same person as in the Palmerston North issue. Again, we didn't know what was going on at first because there was no legal compulsion for us to be told, but once more, God intervened so that we could be involved and ensure the situation was managed well.

In this situation, a church in Christchurch submitted a resolution to Charities Services to change the trust deeds, essentially giving the senior pastor, who was driving this change, lifetime input into how the financial interests and assets were managed, and removing ACTS governance completely. Because the resolution was signed by the senior minister, all the elders, and the five board members including the overseer, he could have gotten away with it legally.

Thankfully, God intervened, and Charities Services sent a letter to our national office notifying us that changes had been made to the trust deed. We then went away and found out what the changes were and approached the church only to be told in no uncertain tone that according to the new terms of the local trust, we had no control or legal authority over the place. This was technically correct, because, at that point, there was no consultation clause in place. We asked the church to reverse the changes, but they wouldn't.

We talked to our lawyer who informed us we had no comeback. "You've got nothing," he said. "They have five trustees, and they've all signed the document."

At the council meeting that followed, something rose in me. I knew in my spirit that what we were facing was deeply wrong. I was upset about what had happened, but I knew God was even more grieved by this corrupt behaviour. Asking the twenty-one members of the council to stand, I said, "We're going to do something now, and if you don't agree with me, I want you to leave the room for a moment. I'm going to pray, and I want one hundred percent unity so we can break the spirit of corruption that's taken hold in this situation. What's happened in Christchurch is not God-honouring. It needs to be stopped." Everyone stayed, and we prayed together, contending against the spirit involved and breaking the schemes of the enemy that were in play within this situation. We then officially removed the credentials of the overseer and the senior leader and advised the church that it was no longer part of the ACTS movement.

The repercussions of this were immediate, and far bigger than I anticipated. For some reason, it caused great havoc. The next day I received a call from one of the local board members—also a credentialled pastor—in Christchurch. "I'm sorry," he said, "What I've done is wrong and I'm prepared to rectify things however I can." The next day I got a call from a second board member saying the same thing. Less than twenty-four hours later I was sitting at the airport when someone I thought was too onside with the others to have any contrary thought, also called me. He simply said, "I'm so sorry. I will support you in the meeting."

As a National Leadership Team, we had decided our connection with this church was finished. In our minds, we were on our way to a meeting in Christchurch to finalise the relationship. Yet by the time we got to this meeting, three trustees had voluntarily repented. The balance of the situation had shifted toward honouring the movement. Finally, the overseer also admitted his approach had not been right. This isolated the senior pastor who had initiated the changes, and we were able to dismiss him right away.

It was phenomenal watching this scenario unfold, as the gentle but persistent hand of God moved us all toward a resolution to the crisis. In the end, the church didn't leave the movement. Instead, they dismissed the pastor, revoked the changes to the trust deeds, and came back under the umbrella of ACTS. We found another senior leader for that church, and the council worked with the overseer personally until we were able to restore his standing and re-credential him. From then on, we determined to watch for similar dynamics so we could move in quicker and help bring resolution and healing, and even mediation if necessary.

This was an unfortunate incident. It's one of those events where you look back and wish it didn't have to happen, but in hindsight, you discover how helpful it actually was. It taught me that we can intervene in prayer and get answers very quickly and effectively overnight. God was very good. Both situations provided an impetus to change a clause in the partnership manual before anything like this could ever happen again. From that point on, it was written into the partnership manual that the overseeing minister was obliged to consult with the National Leadership Team on any change of practice, and that all ACTS churches must adhere to the template for trusts that we had created. That made us more secure as a movement going forward. From then on, there was a growing sense that my job was effectively finished.

SAM TAKES OVER

Going into the council meeting at the end of 2016, I didn't have the future mapped out. Although it was an election year, Helen and I hadn't discussed whether I would stand for the role of National Leader once more, or come to any conclusions together. We were both just there in the meeting when I got a firm sense that the work I had been called to accomplish as the leader of the ACTS movement was finished. Speaking to the council, I said, "I won't be standing for re-election."

This was unexpected because I had earlier intimated that I wanted to serve for another term. I could have stayed on, but I knew in my spirit that I had completed what God had given me to do and that my time was over.

One thing Helen and I often comment on is our ability to accurately discern and anticipate a change in season. A lot of leaders struggle with this, but throughout our lives, we have been graced to know when it is time to move on and to act accordingly. Looking back, I am grateful we made that call. It was the right time for Sam to step up and lead.

NEW LEADERSHIP

Sam was already on the council, and at that meeting, the council unanimously chose him to assume the role of national leader in my place. He wasn't appointed by me, but I knew, and the council could see, that he was ready. Part of being elected involves articulating your vision to the group. Sam did that magnificently, and his vision complemented the journey we had been on. This was important because a new leader can launch the movement in an entirely new direction, which can be difficult for all involved. That was true when I took up the position as national leader, but over sixteen years we had developed a streamlined process, incrementally taking ground.

As Sam took the helm, the momentum continued. He built on what we had accomplished under my leadership, and it was a strong and steady transition into a safe set of hands. He had been close to the action all along and knew what had gone into building us to that point. Sam has achieved great things since then, and the current direction is very much his. I'm grateful, because the legacy of my leadership has never been undermined. It continues to this day as a foundation for something fresh and vital, and there is no sense of wasted effort on my part, although this can happen easily enough.

I have the attitude that everything must always be open to being challenged. Looking back, I think we did things well within the framework and the season we found ourselves in. We did what we thought was right. Even so, I don't presume to think that any changes made in my period of leading the movement could not be further challenged. If I heard that Sam and the National Leadership Team were intending to head off in an entirely new direction, I wouldn't take that personally, because times continue to change, and vision is always unfolding.

The last thing you want in leadership is for vision to get stale. You continually need to refresh the structure, so that it serves the vision for that particular time. Structure serves vision, and it must be constantly tuned and honed to ensure it is a good fit. I would not like us to retreat into what we've fought to come out of, and I would probably speak up if that happened, but given the widespread conviction and confidence among both staff and members regarding the current structure, I can't see that as a likely possibility.

Today, we see the evidence all around us—evidence that we got it right and implemented it well. People are flourishing, energised, and free to take ground. Things are flowing organically. Leadership at the local level is empowered, and the fears that we had to push through to get to this point have faded away. It was a lot of work but we got there together, and there is deep ownership of the structure and model. The difficulties are behind us, and we have found a healthy groove in which to operate and flourish.

15

Fresh Horizons

While I held the position of national leader, I gave a lot of energy to the role. I carried a great deal of responsibility, and there was so much to juggle at any one time. Stepping down after sixteen years was a significant moment for me. We all go through life in stages, and I needed to ask what was next for myself, and for Helen and I as a couple.

FATHERING IN THE NATIONS

Sam wanted to focus on New Zealand, but he asked if I would continue to represent ACTS internationally and also remain as the 'apostolic father' over what we had established with Equippers overseas.

That invitation, which I accepted, has helped me transition. I'm so very grateful for that. After serving as the ACTS movement's national leader for eight terms, it was satisfying to not step into a vacuum. My new role allows me to think globally the entire time, which is so life-giving for someone like me who is wired strategically. From the year 2000 until the outbreak of Covid-19, I spent six months every year outside New Zealand, travelling around Equippers churches and supporting them however I could.

It has always been in my heart to foster the development and maturity of apostles around the world. One of the most enjoyable opportunities I have had in recent years has been to create an international apostolic forum. We have intentionally limited this to around forty delegates made up of ACTS

Church leaders and their teams, ensuring an intimate environment where everyone can get to know each other and be comfortable and open in each other's company. I have had the opportunity to chair this forum, which has been a blessing to me as well.

When we meet as an international apostolic forum, we discuss a whole range of topics, like individual apostolic initiatives, releasing the emerging generation, being missional, how National Leadership Teams function, and leadership in general. This group has always been generous toward me, and even though I am older now, they continue to endorse me as their chairman. Among our international churches there has been plenty of opportunity for me to preach, but I have naturally been drawn to the role of coming alongside the pastors and leaders, sitting with them and talking about the issues they are facing, how those issues can be addressed, and how we might strengthen the church so that it becomes a manifestation of the vision they carry.

Since stepping down from the National Leadership in NZ, it has been such a joy to be part of the lifeblood of ACTS and Equippers, and to continue to have a leadership role. However, Covid-19 brought fresh challenges, and the perspectives that arose from that have been able to serve us better still.

DEVELOPING INDEPENDENCE

Prior to Covid-19, much of what was happening with Equippers internationally was, in retrospect, probably centred too much around myself—and particularly my visits. With unforeseen lockdowns, our leaders were suddenly thrown into the deep end. With no preparation time, the weight fell on their shoulders, and they were forced to take responsibility for themselves and adapt while answering difficult questions like, "What does this mean for us?" and "How can we multiply, grow and develop in our own right?"

In facing the challenges of Covid-19, the vast majority of our international leaders rose to another level in their discernment with God. This resulted in the creation of deeply rooted and wonderfully powerful apostolic houses as our leaders apprehended what God was doing and recognised the importance of maintaining healthy connections. In this regard, I believe the interruption to the status quo served rather than hindered what God was doing. Coming out of Covid restrictions and connecting again, I observe a greater level of maturity within us all. We've now got apostolic leaders 'owning' their nation with its own culture, idiosyncrasies and issues, as a personal challenge, and developing vision under God that is expansive enough and innovative enough for substantial kingdom impact. Seeing this makes the father's heart I carry overjoyed.

For our international leaders, the moment when they realised that the future lay within them was pivotal. This is true for all apostles—you must come to a point where you realise that your authority as an apostle is enough, and while you honour and value leadership over you, you are no longer looking to others to fix the problem in front of you. You are an *apostle,* and together with the Holy Spirit, you can carry vision and become a catalyst for breakthrough within your area of influence. You can gather people, nurture leaders, and truly blaze a trail in your own right. The future lies within you, it lies within your community, within the apostolic initiative.

It is unhealthy for an apostle to be always looking to the outside; it can even be a distraction. Since the Covid period, our leaders have stepped up and engaged in their own right, and as a movement, Equippers has grown internationally. We now have churches in fifteen countries and fifty locations around the world, along with several hubs that strengthen and multiply our reach. Our leaders in London, Germany and Italy have also developed training institutions, creating contexts where churches and their emerging leaders can grow and mature more rapidly.

APOSTOLIC HOUSES

Both internationally and in New Zealand, Sam has brought incredible strength into the movement. One of the areas that has developed under his leadership is the role of the overseeing minister. What started as an idea is now a fully-fledged part of who we are as a movement and how we function. Our churches are beginning to recognise, understand and own the importance of the overseeing minister role. The SHOUT conference has also grown. What started as a local church conference is now a national gathering that draws leaders and their ministry teams as well as their churches together from around the country.

Other movements have begun looking in with a desire to become part of what's happening. Recently, an entire group of churches joined the ACTS movement. They are fully adopting our way of doing things and our culture, and all their ministers are now credentialled by ACTS. We are seeing the same dynamic overseas. People and churches are joining in and loving the environment we provide, which allows initiatives to flourish and grow.

As well as this, we are seeing the development of more and more apostolic houses. Right now, this initiative is moving faster overseas than it is in New Zealand, but it is being strengthened with each successive emerging generation. Some leaders are good at managing or adopting what already exists, but it takes an entirely different calibre of apostolic leader to initiate something new and raise leadership around that. When that happens, a new apostolic house is created, and you have effectively reproduced. This is a powerful dynamic with missional momentum that impacts the nations and seeds revival. In New Zealand, we are seeing significant apostolic leaders rise from the generation who are now coming into their thirties.

An apostolic house is bigger than a single apostle with their own initiative. These houses form when apostles of different gifting come together, some to break new ground and some to safeguard and tend what is already in place. Apostolic leaders flourish when they are connected with other apostolic leaders. This is called 'apostolic collegiality'—when they come together, they spur one another on to do great things for God. That's the strength of what we're trying to establish through Equippers around the world. We want to create apostolic houses, one after another. This promotes growth because we are not constrained by the need to be connected with a single visionary centre and resource pool. These apostolic houses are self-sufficient in a way that ensures we are keeping resources, training and support as close as possible to where they are used. An illustration we come back to a lot is, "You can count the seeds in an orange, but only God knows the number of oranges in that seed." Each apostolic house is a seed. They are small, but if they grow, they can multiply. I often think, "How many churches or kingdom initiatives are in the heart of one apostolic leader who understands this dynamic?"

We are starting to see this season of flourishing in our movement. If we saw ourselves as one apostolic house worldwide, we would only be reinventing what we have come out of and become institutionalised once again. Instead, we are pushing outward while maintaining connection. For Equippers, the Auckland church was a strong apostolic house from which everything was seeded in the early days. The same is now true of London, Rome, Manila, Calcutta, Mainz, Flensburg, Berlin, Budapest, and the central coast of the United States. We are also seeing emerging apostolic houses in Switzerland, Mexico, Brazil, and Tonga.

Since then, something exciting has developed. Our apostolic houses are looking around and seeing ways in which they can collaborate and support one another. The Central Coast has adopted Mexico and is serving and helping them. Mainz is doing the same for Brazil, as is London for Ghana.

In this way, resources are flowing from one demographic to another, allowing us to put in place ministries that would have taken many years to establish if every city was left to itself. Instead, apostles in low socioeconomic contexts can step into their calling and breakthrough, empowered by resources from somewhere else in the world, where funds are easier to obtain. As we build a multi-apostolic-house situation, we can expect to see fresh waves of higher-level strategic vision like this emerging.

KEY STRATEGIES

One apostolic house can't carry enough vision for everyone or resource everyone, but by cooperating together we can get the job done. As funds flow from one apostolic house to the next and one country to another, opportunities arise to execute key strategies in places where a lack of resources might have strangled growth for years.

This is especially the case when it comes to *education and training*. If we're in the business of developing the call of God on people's lives, there is no better place than a classroom to see that happen. An education centre can bless a region until individual training facilities can be set up later. This was the case for our London training centre. Emerging leaders from Europe initially travelled to the United Kingdom for training, and today, training facilities in Mainz and Rome are forming. This kind of work can be very demanding. The apostolic leader must be careful not to create a program too quickly, because getting the correct calibre of curriculum and teachers takes time to establish. Nevertheless, whenever one of our apostolic houses opens a location-based Bible school, we start to see real traction occur in that region.

Our *conferences* are also key. Within ACTS, our annual conference is a very important way for our people to stay connected. We also organise two or three gatherings throughout the year, bringing pastors and leaders into an environment where they can talk and also be ministered to and prayed for. As part of Equippers, we have also established pastor's forums with a similar purpose. As Equippers has grown internationally, our knowledge of the significance and effectiveness of gathering our people together has motivated us to create conferences similar to SHOUT for our people outside of New Zealand. We now have two major annual conferences, one in New Zealand, and the other one held in Europe. Big gatherings can open the hearts of people to a great move of God!

Another key for us is our *relationship with other movements*. So far, God has provided the opportunity for us to cross-pollinate with apostolic movements in Denmark, Switzerland and Australia. A similar relationship is beginning to form with the church in Ghana. Likewise, Equippers churches in both Slovakia and Hungary have opened doors for us to engage with the apostolic church in their region.

THE VALUE OF TRAVEL

My primary passion now is to see Equippers continue to multiply and to do what I can to support our apostolic leaders to grow personally and to expand the scope of their vision and influence. This involves a lot of international travel. If all the Equippers pastors and leaders in a region are coming together, I try to be there to meet with them in person. For example, a leaders' gathering in Italy might start on a Friday night and continue the following day. I may be asked to minister as part of the program—and I'm often asked to preach at one of their churches on the Sunday afterwards—but that's not why I'm there. Most importantly, it is a chance to sit down with pastors and talk with them. It's a valuable opportunity to support leaders in the wider context.

As chair of the international Apostolic forum, I travel to those gatherings, and this usually leads to an opportunity to minister in other environments. There always seems to be a major event or two happening somewhere nearby, and if I receive an invitation, I let others within a few hours of travel know that I am available if they would like me to minister in any way that is helpful to them. My itinerary just evolves from there.

Travelling is important because it allows me to develop quality relationships with significant leaders on behalf of the movement. God has supported me in building meaningful relationships with many leaders globally, and I think that will continue to increase because our ethos is not to simply decide that we're going to plant a church in a particular place. Instead, as significant people with ability and desire come into a relationship with us, something takes root, and with this synergy, God works to extend His kingdom.

Great culture multiplies, and apostolic houses carry such culture. It works, people value it, they own it, and they want to see it replicated. Great culture is also resilient because it keeps everyone connected and promotes health throughout the community. This is why, whenever a spirit of independence comes in, it needs to be addressed. When we take an independent stance, it is easy to lose ground.

When we concentrate on shaping culture, we can build something that is attractive to others. We must ensure there is a positive tone, good vision, leadership and credibility, and the atmosphere needs to be pastoral, with a high care factor to see everyone thriving. When our people are flourishing, we can start to get excited, because our structure is serving the most important aspect of church, the release of people. That's the real testimony that God is at work among us.

It is evident our culture is working when people want to join us, and this applies to groups as well. In New Zealand, our movement has a very good relationship with other movements like Elim and New Life. When they look on and see good culture, it is viewed as complementary to what they are also seeking to do.

Attracting and releasing people is an important dynamic in the kingdom. Our national leader in Ghana understood this. Realising they were losing the next generation, he sent three young people to our college. The plan was that they would return to Accra, where one or two of them would plant another church, creating a model like ours that would stretch the existing church to change. The hope was that a new apostolic wave of initiative would seed growth and life for them again. In my mind, this is the kind of thinking that works.

Today, my role is to father others. I loved transforming our movement, and all the responsibility, detail, effort, administration and strategic thinking that this entailed. My passion is to come alongside significant people and help them think strategically, but I have no desire to tell them what to do. My mission and mandate are about seeing Christ formed in people, and that is entirely relational. It is about connecting deeply, having kingdom influence, and most of all, seeing successive generations continue to love and serve Jesus.

16

Mission Debrief

For a long time—since the late eighties—I carried a three-pronged vision for the ACTS movement. This was always crystal clear to me. It was also a very personal mandate. After leading the movement for sixteen years, it seems appropriate to take stock and reflect on the degree to which it has come to pass.

The first 'prong' of the vision was to create an environment for apostolic initiatives to prosper and freely find expression. The second was to release an emerging generation so that they could develop a passion for leadership and find the call of God on their lives. The third was to foster kingdom expression within our community. These aspirations have underpinned my entire contribution and have been a driving force behind all our reforms. But how have they fared?

AN ENVIRONMENT FOR APOSTOLIC INITIATIVES

When we look around at what has been accomplished, it is clear that ownership at a local level continues to flourish. Churches are taking responsibility for their locality and their God-given contribution there. What began with the pastors has cascaded out to the leaders and members of our churches. As people developed and matured into greater responsibility, their levels of faith have risen too, because in taking ownership and outworking a vision, faith will always be challenged and stretched. Since

God rewards faith, this in itself creates even more momentum.

The old hierarchical model created frustration and blame. Now that responsibility is in local hands, there's no one else to point the finger at. If something's not working, the local community needs to come together to prayerfully solve any problems that exist. That pushes them toward collaboration, creativity and courage, and the results have been amazing. We've seen a multiplication of resources, and the expansion of our mission scope and impact as a movement is beyond anything we expected or even thought possible in the early years.

Organic growth at a local level continues to seed leadership talent. As local churches have discovered the rich array of leadership potential within, there has been an upturn in the calibre and strength of emerging leadership and we are finding that each successive generation has more to offer. In this way, the risks previously voiced about pushing accountability nearer to the coalface and supporting local empowerment have been answered.

Our local churches have come of age. We have been delighted to see what they have become and also diligent to ensure they succeeded. There have been very real challenges, but the movement has wrapped around the local leadership with support and training so that they have all the information and help they require. Individuals and churches are flourishing in an environment that fosters significant contributions, great relationships, and mutuality. Others have looked on with interest, attracted to what they see. They have begun to say, "We don't want to do it alone anymore. This would be a good place to belong. There's enough here for us to both add and receive something in the mix. We could find expression here and it's not going to impinge on our vision." Every time another church has joined ACTS, we have benefited too, but that is always secondary to the mutual blessing. In this way, the positive flow-on effects continue.

These factors have been in play for a considerable period now, and strong apostolic houses have formed. We are now seeing a healthy movement birth the beginning of an entirely new one with the same growth potential again. An apostolic house can bring strategic alignment, and represents the difference between a random kind of 'church plonking' and real 'church planting'. It is when each new initiative is deeply rooted, with great leadership, accountability, adequate resources and vision, that longevity and sustainability are assured.

RELEASING AN EMERGING GENERATION

If we want an emerging generation to be set on fire for God, the youth need to be trusted while they find their identity and expression. With this in mind, a lot of our events have been intentionally handed to the youth. These young adults hold rallies, give altar calls, and witness hundreds raise their hands to receive Jesus. It's not just an ideal. It is us actively engaging with our future, and it has been such an inspiration to see it working so well.

An example of this is our Revolution Tour, which Jordan Smith pioneered and is continuing to move from strength to strength. This initiative has become a trusted platform within New Zealand schools, allowing us to speak wisdom to social issues like bullying and other dilemmas kids may be struggling with. We create an atmosphere that is compassionate and affirming, and many of the students have felt comfortable enough to come to a subsequent Revolution Tour meeting at one of our churches. Often this marks the beginning of a young person's journey of faith with us—a journey of building their potential leadership and setting them up for a life of significant contribution.

Our local youth are also amazing. One girl in her twenties who is in our church pulled together a twenty-four-hour prayer meeting with fifty other young people joining her. Others meet to pray at the gate of their high schools before their day starts. They hold events called 'Uprisings' where they create fun environments for their peers with amazing music and altar calls that always draw a great response toward Jesus. It is so meaningful for me to see this kind of activity because I first responded to Jesus in a similar environment as a young person with a life and way of thinking that was less than godly. When youth initially engage with us in these settings, we soon find them attending church. Once God gets on the inside of us, He can do so much more. Change doesn't happen overnight but when youth lead other youth in discipleship contexts, this creates pathways for them to grow and progress in their relationship with Jesus.

We also see the potential in our children, and we invest in them. Helen has an amazing perspective on this. She believes and teaches that "Children's ministry is not just a place where kids are entertained, but a place of equipping children to grow in their relationship with Christ where they are comfortable in prayer, praise, worship, and sharing their faith." In our churches, children are taught to pray and prophesy. They're getting baptised in the Holy Spirit at a young age, and they are finding expression for their particular gifting. When children recognise that Christianity is not just for the adults, but that they are vital members of the church, they see it as a place where they can belong and contribute. This is so important. When I look around today, I see the promise of the emerging generation. I am convinced that the apostolic calling will be in good hands with them. This second prong of my vision is like the first. It starts small but as it advances, it accelerates in a way that manifests the incredible power of God.

KINGDOM CULTURE AND EXPRESSION

The third pillar of my vision speaks to the importance of kingdom expression as individuals find and pursue the mandate for their lives within community. We surround and support each other as we each engage—and eventually succeed—in what God has given us individually to do. When we embody kingdom values together, people can thrive and begin penetrating the world in highly specific and inspired ways. Two or more people with the same assignment may join forces to have a more significant impact on our world than they could achieve alone. Sometimes our mission is more than a personal one, and collaboration is required to achieve our collective potential.

Kingdom expression is found when we show up to challenges within society and let ourselves be agents of God's creative genius together, but individual formation is also key. I find this concept very exciting. Those who carry a clear vision must retain a single-minded focus on nurturing and growing their inner life. This becomes a bridge for them to find their place in the world and to live for Jesus in the way He designed for them. Going deeper with Christ is essential. If we are to play our part in establishing His kingdom here on earth as it is in heaven, then we need to be intimately connected to the one whose kingdom it is.

Kingdom expression can be difficult to measure, but we have observed three key trends that happen when individuals are supported to live out their purpose. In general, we are seeing an increased uptake in education, church planting, and local church involvement. In terms of education, our ministry schools are drawing and empowering students from around the world. Church planting is also thriving, with each new community carrying the potential to become a hub or support centre for further kingdom expression. And in terms of local church involvement, increased ownership is driving higher levels of participation. People are stepping up, and our hope is that the confidence and personal growth that comes from this will spill out of our churches to transform the secular realm. We want our people to be 'truly themselves' and to represent what we are as a community to those who have never experienced the beauty of kingdom culture.

FLOURISHING

Looking back, our people were once frustrated but now they are flourishing. They are coming alive and expressing a deeper inner life. There's a greater awareness of the potential of every member and the gifts they carry. Instead of people losing motivation because they are only seen as a support for someone else's gift, we have created an environment where every gift of grace is valued. This has been communicated and demonstrated, and because our members feel valued, a season of flourishing has begun for them.

This is also the case for our leaders and five-fold ministers. We used to over-value the apostolic gifting, but now we have created a culture where pastors, teachers, prophets and evangelists have truly taken their place among us. Many have been freed from embracing gift profiles that didn't fit comfortably. Steve Graham, as an example of this, is now recognised as a teacher and his influence is global. With his gift, he has made a valuable individual contribution, taking biblical wisdom and revelation and bringing structure and language to our movement.

We are also now starting to see the emergence of the evangelist. The evangelists among us are beginning to say, "Wow! I can flourish here! I don't need to be running evangelistic events on my own. I can serve, I can gather people, I can function in this environment." Those with pastoral gifts are realising that they are essential to the growth and maturity of everyone in our community. Likewise, prophets have begun to find their place. The clarity they carry is valued among us, and as a movement, we recognise that they reinforce the vision in a way so crucial for the wellbeing of all our apostolic initiatives.

A PLACE OF SAFETY

Some of our people have a strong leadership style. Others are creative or gentle, pastoral or patient. It is wonderful to now see our environment making room for a diversity of leadership styles. Helen and I have a unique kind of authority, and for a long time we used that to protect our leaders from the structural limitations of the last season. Even before we reformed the movement we were able to empower, resource and release others to lead.

A leader doesn't have to fix everything to create a significant bubble of safety in which their people can flourish, but because we had that opportunity and acted on it, all types of leaders of different strengths can now flourish within ACTS. Considering the hard work so many put in to implement the changes, it is a little amusing when some of our leaders say, "You made all of these changes, but we didn't feel much difference!" But it is also encouraging because it demonstrates that the movement now does what Helen and I once did for them. It is a surprising legacy, and now, as successive generations of leaders raise others under them, they do not need to exert themselves against the environment in order to thrive because the environment is conducive to a wonderful medley of people and leaders flourishing together.

Building what we have today took legal work, administration, and many people making a personal contribution, but there was also a battle to fight against forces that oppose great culture and individual contribution. We each have a small part to play, but we don't underestimate the power of God to weave together our victories into something greater. The battle is His responsibility, and He is sufficient in the face of it, so there is no need for a leader to go to bed anxious and exhausted. When we use our strength to create safety for others, they see the wins, they see what's possible, and they feel safe and protected. There is a kind of hope and momentum an entire army gains when they realise they are on the winning side. This advantage feeds on itself. Our task is to build environments the Holy Spirit is attracted to, and when He functions among us, we all flourish.

We can also take ground in this fight by deliberately expressing thankfulness, even when our circumstances seem contrary. In other words, we choose to bring a whole heart of worship before God, even when we may not feel like it. It is our deliberate choice to put off the garment of heaviness and clothe ourselves with grace and praise that overcomes the giants that oppose us.

Finally, we know the power of prayer. There is something about the posture of prayer that calibrates us to the lightness and joy of a war already won. We walk in Christ's victory, and it manifests in our leadership. When we ride upon the waves that radiate from Christ's ultimate triumph against the darkness, others want to join us. Now there is less darkness and more light in the world! The Holy Spirit ministers among us, creating a growing community of people with an overcoming culture who are alive to God.

HUNGER AND HABITS

So much has been achieved, and in our hearts, we want it all to stand the test of time. When I see our young people, I know that the future is secure. My teenage years were a bit rocky, but later there became a hunger in me to grow. Nowadays, I look for that in others—people who are motivated and determined to realign anything in their lives that is out of sync with the culture of Jesus. When people have that attitude, things start to happen. Change comes for them and those around them. We don't want legalism in our churches. The Holy Spirit is all we need, and the hunger is from Him. When we see hunger, it is evidence of His presence, and if we invest in such people, they can weather the entire journey, persevere on a leadership track, and become champions of the environment we have set.

Through the Holy Spirit, God is fashioning us from the inside out into the image of His Son. We have the anointing on us, but we also have the anointing *in us,* teaching us and changing us. It is one thing to have a flourishing environment, but without an inherent hunger, the generational momentum of what we have achieved will slow and we could even drift back in the direction we have come.

True hunger expresses itself in our manner of life, our choices, and our habits. It comes out in our homes and workplaces, our marriages and relationships, our spending habits, our desires, our thought life, and how we spend our time. It is a fire that permeates our lifestyle when it burns within us. Habits are important, and a great measure of whether holy fire is operating in us is the degree to which our lives are centred around relationships with God and others.

Are we actively engaged in relationships where we evidence the fruits of the Spirit? Do we react to disappointment by leaning toward or retreating from others? Are we collecting people in our lives as a valuable commodity, and are we pursuing increasing levels of trust and vulnerability with them? When hunger draws out discipline in us, our habits are reshaped and our lifestyles testify to the reality that Jesus has truly been formed in us.

PART FOUR

PRINCIPLES AND PRACTICE

17

What Do I See?

Our son Hamish is an exceptional architect. Many years ago, he designed a house for Helen and I. He had a vision, but he also consulted with us and engaged with our ideas. Next, he shared conceptual drawings and architectural blueprints with the builder who would be entrusted with bringing about the vision he saw. As the project progressed, Hamish articulated the vision in greater detail, explaining what was involved so that the builders and all their contractors could truly engage with the project. The result was simply brilliant.

As an apostle, I am in the role of master builder. I carry the vision, then I bring it to the community, and we execute it together. The Holy Spirit is the architect of the entire kingdom of Jesus Christ, and I need to be continually in step with Him for my work and for our contribution as a community to take shape just the way God the Father intended. It is no good for me to try and deduce vision or work it out using logic or even principles I know have worked well elsewhere. Vision is specific to a particular situation, and what the Holy Spirit shows us holds a powerfully prophetic promise that guides us and guarantees that as we pursue *what we see,* it will manifest tangibly before us over time. Vision is without substitute in this regard.

VISION IS ESSENTIAL

The Bible says that without vision, the people perish (Proverbs 29:18). When vision is lacking, people wander around lost without any way to move forward. It is common in churches and in life to find people who cannot see their future and consequently don't know what they are doing or where they are going. We had an example of this in our movement many years before I was leading it. Some of the leaders were thinking about how we could grow, and it was reasoned that if we planted a certain number of churches over a specified timeframe, the movement would grow to 20,000 members. That was what was proposed to the board, and it was an attractive idea at the time. The group then suggested possible locations for each of these new churches. It made sense, but it wasn't a vision, and consequently, it didn't work for us.

It is a true saying that you cannot build it unless you can see it, but vision, when it is present, is also a powerful self-fulfilling force. It is a fire in the belly of the apostle that is only quenched as they move forward, but it is not up to him or her to accomplish the vision they carry because the Holy Spirit who gave it is ultimately responsible, and He makes a way for it to be fulfilled.

I had a vision for our movement long before I could do anything about it, but I was inhibited by the structure and institution around us. That was a frustrating and uncomfortable time for me because I couldn't find a way forward but eventually, openings came. It was seeing the vision ahead of time that ensured I engaged with those opportunities, and in the end, we have come to see the vision fulfilled.

What has God put in your heart? What do you see? What are you prepared to lay your life down for? Later in the process we engage our mind, but first we must see in the Spirit! We are often confronted with something that is not as it should be, some kind of issue that bothers us, but it is not a math problem to solve or a plan to work out. Instead, we should take our concerns before God in prayer and wait for Him to give us a simple and clear picture of what He would like to fashion out of the situation. Vision is a word spoken out of the mouth of our Father that will not fall to the ground. It must take form, and therefore it is an irreplaceable starting point for our breakthrough.

VISION AND ENCOUNTER

Moses received the pattern for Jewish national life directly from God. He also received the exact blueprints for the tabernacle. One was for a legal framework. The other was for a tent. Noah received the plans for a boat. Joshua saw a plan to break into an impenetrable city. These men were all facing the impossible, and they each saw something that unlocked their situations. But think of the variety and the unlikely nature of each vision when it was first shown. It's beyond reason. You can't work it out, and you can't deduce it. Some people think they can strategise or call together a committee to plan, but my observation is that none of that works. The Holy Spirit puts within someone a vision, whether it's to reach a community, build a church or touch a nation, and this is needed before we begin the journey toward a solution. The nature of the vision God wants to entrust to us is powerfully redemptive, but if you can't see it, you and your people can't build it.

It is no coincidence that Scripture refers to Noah—who received a profound vision from God—as having 'found favour' with Him (Genesis 6:8). To see a vision of what God intends to do is a great gift of grace in our lives. God's favour also opens the door to a visitation where we receive promises and miracles that will inevitably change the world. This dynamic is best seen in the life of Mary who found favour and then experienced both an encounter and a miracle of conception—and we all know the world-transforming nature of the rest of the story.

VISION IS PROGRESSIVE

I always knew that God had given me an apostolic grace, and this was initially constrained by the institution I was part of in the mid-nineties. I became frustrated with their view of my gift because I knew there was more in me than what they imagined. I still felt this way when I went on sabbatical but when I came back, I had a divine encounter with God. The Holy Spirit spoke clearly to me out of two passages of Scripture.

First, God showed me that He wanted to enlarge my heart so that I could embrace what He had for me, just as He did for Solomon as he was ascending to his throne:

> *And God gave Solomon wisdom and exceedingly great understanding, **and largeness of heart** like the sand on the seashore.*
>
> — 1 KINGS 4:29

As I started to pray those words, I was struck by another verse:

> *Again and again they tempted God, and **limited the Holy One of Israel.***
>
> — PSALM 78:41

As I read that particular verse, I felt the Holy Spirit focus my attention on the word 'limited' and on the unbelief that was behind it. Then I went into a dream in which I died. I found myself in heaven facing Jesus, and as I looked at Him, He said, "Bruce, I've never doubted your love for me, it's clear to me. But while you were on earth, you limited me. I wanted to do far more in and through your life."

I woke and felt crushed by the fact that I had held back on what God wanted to do. The words from my dream blended the two scriptures for me: I was limiting God, and since He wanted to do far more with me, He was going to build new and greater capacity in me!

This was compelling because I had seen something that clarified what God intended for my life. I knew that I needed to reposition myself to fully engage with opportunities to contribute in the future. The truth was, without seeing that, I would never have been receptive to Him stretching the scope of our work to include an international reach. Instead, I opened myself to the Holy Spirit and was ready when God visited me less than a month later with a more specific vision.

When I was on a plane reading the in-flight magazine and received this vision, I noticed the network map for that airline showed flight paths heading in all directions around the globe. In the vision God gave me, the map changed to convey ten cities in ten countries arising from red curved lines emanating out of Auckland.

This was another meeting with God, and it provided further clarity about what God wanted to do. He had already spoken to me, but now I had *seen* His desires for us. From that moment on, I carried a vision that was more specific and detailed. I also came away from that experience freshly motivated. I had heard so clearly from God! He had told me He would enlarge my heart, and now, less than a month later, He had elaborated on the plan so that I was no longer thinking it was only about New Zealand. Now I wondered, what would it look like if the vision was global, and how would we get it done? As we grappled with our strategy, that meeting with God gave us a wonderful point of focus. We had the blueprint we needed for Equippers to come alive!

For me, vision is progressive. It unfolds as we engage with it. As we tried to stretch beyond our natural borders with our apostolic initiative, the hierarchical structure of the Apostolic Church movement became a huge obstacle. Finding ways to move forward with the overseas part of our vision took great perseverance, but the tension and hindrances we encountered eventually led to the first prong of the three-fold vision I possessed when I later became the national leader of our movement.

I knew our structure needed to change if I was to fully implement what I'd been given, so everything we did during those years was a natural outworking of my earlier vision. Thankfully, in freeing up our own vision we were freeing up other leaders to follow through on the blueprints they too had received.

What came next became extremely foundational for Helen and me—and for all of Equippers. As I was reading Isaiah, the Lord said that I should pray some particular verses over myself. In the weeks that followed these words 'got under my skin' and became part of me:

> *He made my mouth like a sharpened sword, in the shadow of his hand he hid me; he made me into **a polished arrow** and concealed me **in his quiver**.*

> *This is what the Lord says: "In the time of my favor I will answer you, and in the day of salvation I will help you; I will keep you and will make you to be a covenant for the people, to restore the land and to reassign its desolate inheritances, to say to the captives, 'Come out,' and to those in darkness, 'Be free!'"*
>
> — *Isaiah 49:2, 8-9 NIV*

The arrow and quiver informed my understanding of the picture of ten cities emanating out from Auckland. I saw the curved lines as red arrows loosed from our largest city, streaking out to impact ten other major centres throughout the world. Vision pictures speak so much to the nuances of our thinking and help us implement what we have seen. Most of the work and care in releasing an arrow is done at the origin rather than the destination, and there is an inevitability to what happens after it is let fly. I could see that our aim, draw, and the make of our arrows would be important to the outcomes we would experience.

I kept praying the words of Isaiah 49, and in the days leading up to our first Wednesday-night prayer meeting in the Auckland church, the idea of 'calling people out of darkness' and 'setting people free from prison' had become a point of focus. That night as we prayed, those words were at the top of my mind. We began to pray for the youth and the emerging generations when suddenly I received another vision! This time, I watched as God turned 'the prisoners' and 'the ones in darkness' from a nameless collection of needy souls into a group I could recognise. I came away from that encounter knowing that I was to lead the emerging generation out of darkness and set them free!

This was the beginning of what would later become the second prong of my vision as the national leader. Along the way, I realised that the youth themselves are the best ones to set other youth free and that the most effective way to run with this vision was to equip them and then move aside so they could rise into that role. I kept praying Isaiah 49, putting more focus on the youth, and from this we quickly began to see results. Vision is the irreplaceable powerful force behind breakthrough for us all, and it was now in play. I saw more and more young people flourishing in the house of God. When Cindy Jacobs later came to New Zealand, she prophesied over us saying, "This movement will create an environment for young firebrands to be raised up." This became a significant confirming prophecy for us and demonstrated the essential relationship between vision and the prophetic word—one builds on the other.

The Lord's Prayer has always been important to me. Jesus ended that prayer with, "Your kingdom come." This allowed me to be open to what God wanted for us in terms of kingdom significance. There is also a gentle allusion to the kingdom in Isaiah 49, which refers to a covenant that is restorative to the earth. In later years, Isaiah 49 became the basis of our mission statement for Equippers. It is very important to us. My three-pronged vision was still forming at the time, but the foundation had already been laid in my heart and mind that kingdom focus would be an essential part of my vision going forward.

The kingdom-focus component of my vision was strengthened during a sermon I was preaching. As I spoke, I found myself stating very clearly that Jesus' primary mission on earth, aside from what He accomplished on the cross, was to establish the kingdom. We see this throughout the Gospels. All of Jesus' parables and teachings were about the kingdom! This continues in the book of Acts where we find Jesus between His resurrection and ascension,

*. . . speaking of the things **pertaining to the kingdom of God.***

— ACTS 1:3

When Jesus was preparing the early church to take over His kingdom work, He knew they would need the Holy Spirit to continue in His place. As I was preaching, I found myself articulating a kingdom vision with a new message. We would pursue the kingdom in two ways: by planting effective churches that would extend the kingdom of God in their locations, and by educating our people, training them and equipping them for significance wherever they found their fit. This is important because for many years Christians have generally fallen into two schools of thought, but both are necessary. Some tend to be all about 'the kingdom' (such as those involved in YWAM and many student ministries), while others are all about 'the church' (such as most local pastors and church planting movements). What we need to see, however, is the church ushering in the kingdom of God. This is why the church exists. As churches, we have a responsibility to expand the kingdom.

BUILDING WITH VISION

The idea that vision is what we can genuinely *see,* has served me well. I first heard this articulated clearly through Brian Houston. He spoke about, "the church he saw," and I am convinced that the reason he has been able to achieve so much is because what he could *see* in advance was phenomenal. I'm still inspired by those words. My good friend Danny Guglielmucci says something similar. From Exodus 25, he talks about "building according to the pattern"—in other words, "the pattern is what you see".

Paul was a wise master builder. He laid the foundation (1 Corinthians 3) knowing that someone else would come along later to build upon it. He exhorts us to be careful about how we build and the type of materials we use. Some will build with wood, hay and stubble. Others will use gold, silver or precious stones. Quality matters—and to me, that's about people. If you're after gold, look for people with the right attitude. Work with people who have genuine faith that's been tested by fire, people who carry the nature of Christ, people with gifts that are seasoned by the Holy Spirit, useful and enduring. Others may be an easy pick—they're right there, and you can put them to work quickly. But they haven't yet been seasoned by the cross, they haven't been in the fire. They don't display the beauty of Christ. These people may be with you one minute and gone the next. They never become part of the building. At best, they were scaffolding, momentarily useful, but when the building emerges they are no longer on the scene. Danny Guglielmucci often refers to this scripture:

> And the temple, when it was being built, was built with stone finished at the quarry, so that no hammer or chisel or any iron tool was heard in the temple while it was being built.
>
> — 1 KINGS 6:7

There was no noise on the building site because all the work of the chiselling of the stones was done in the quarry! The point is, we first *invest* in people and then we *build* with them.

I love hearing Steve Graham tell the story of how in his early days he saw himself "preaching to a thousand" and "being part of a global movement with ten locations". He had the vision and was strategising in line with that, but it wasn't until twenty years later when he heard me share my vision of ten churches in ten significant cities of the world that he realised he needed to be part of an apostolic company where his 'single finger' could become part of an 'entire hand' that could take hold of what God had shown him.

You may feel as though you only have a rudimentary vision, barely enough to begin. I have found that if we get moving with what we have, more will be revealed as we need it. Vision is progressive. It grows. God will give you the people you need. If you build carefully, according to the pattern, your work will be lasting. If the Holy Spirit is guiding you, you will leave a legacy!

18

Institutional Thinking

There are two sorts of gardeners. Some appreciate order, and shape their idea of beauty through the rigorous use of hedge trimmers and pruning clippers. There is another kind of gardener who enjoys the variety of plant life, with all its colours and contrasts. Their backyards might be a little wild, but the organic and intrinsic beauty of the plants are on display—flowers and foliage are everywhere. Their obsession is to promote growth, to nurture each bush so that their garden teems with life. The same dichotomy exists among those who lead movements. Some are excited about people and their potential, while others, fixated on the system and its agenda, hardly see them at all.

CLOSED-DOOR LEADERSHIP

One of the biggest problems with institutional Christianity is that wonderful people can become locked within a system which they serve, while the potential God has placed in them remains unacknowledged and largely untapped. The people are not truly seen because the institution is at the forefront. The system becomes more important than the people.

This dynamic often shapes the style of leadership that thrives in institutional Christianity. Leaders who champion the system are rewarded with increasing influence, while others are excluded from the conversation. In these environments, decisions are often made behind closed doors in the name of the organisation, with no recourse or forum for the people to be heard. These decisions are usually based on what is good for the institution, rather than on individual conviction. Over time, leaders are chosen because of the degree to which they represent the institution, rather than for their godly character or leadership ability. This isn't a good way to govern, and it does not establish a healthy leadership culture.

Instead, it creates a hierarchical and relational distance, where leaders become unapproachable and questions cannot be asked and answered. The institution has the power to withhold information and resources to control and manipulate its people. At this point, it is easy for religion to take hold—and religion can easily cover sin. Leaders may be able to share in meetings with wisdom and eloquence even when moral failure exists, because sin does not negate the gift. However, hypocrisy leads to pharisaic attitudes, or legalism.

When we build with control in mind, we unconsciously create a beast that soon controls us. One issue comes up after another, and each time we put something in place to prevent a reoccurrence. Then we worry about the possibility of something going wrong and we go further into management mode. On the other hand, properly delegated accountability can become deeply empowering.

Fear is the thread that weaves an institutional web, but we don't often use the word. Instead, we put new policies in place and speak about 'accountability' when it is actually *control* in disguise. Fear was naturally present when we decided to release buildings to our local churches—the fear of losing historical assets. The cost of many years of this fear's rule was that we lost the dynamic of being mobilised and fully alive. The institution was no longer serving the vision or championing the people. This is what happens when structure takes precedence.

PEOPLE LOSING HEART

When people see dysfunction, they lose heart. This often happens when people are appointed to leadership regardless of whether they have slain giants or have a track record of ministering in breakthrough situations.

On the ground, it is unclear why these particular people are making all the decisions and voicing opinions that are beyond scrutiny. They see promotions and appointments based on the institution's needs rather than the gifts of the leaders. It is easy for emerging leaders to get downhearted about this and simply leave the movement because they are disempowered under these conditions. In a more organic environment, heroes rise and lead.

An institution will reward orthodoxy and loyalty, which takes away the necessity to flourish out of a strong inner life. Faith is destroyed under these conditions. How is faith required when the institution can leverage a large pool of assets in order to do more, just like any large corporation would? In this situation, personal engagement and high levels of ownership on the ground are unnecessary. There's no need for anyone to stretch or trust. Sure, it can work, but it costs greatly on a local level because the institution replaces relationship. The moment you remove the need for faith, the whole situation ceases to be pleasing to God.

Of course, when people are starting out, it is helpful to pool resources to help get them going. But once there is traction, the approach needs to change. This may challenge the status quo, but it empowers people and brings momentum. We also need to preserve this momentum by bringing structure that serves the vision, but in doing so, we need to make sure that the refreshed structure is not more important than the vision itself, or Christ, or the people involved. Otherwise, we could have a giant in the making. When our concern for the thing we have built surpasses the purpose we built it for, and we start to introduce measures to protect it even from our own people, the rot has already set in. It will soon become a threat, and a huge battle will be required to resist it and redeem what God originally intended.

FACING A GIANT

We faced a huge battle, and eventually, we won. This was no small accomplishment because the giant of institutionalism was strong and controlling. As we faced off with our Goliath, I had my three-prong vision, like a trident, in hand. We leapt forward, deliberately trying to position our emerging generation where they could be heard. They didn't know this beast that was calling the shots. They instinctively questioned and threatened it. They had fresh ideas and saw no need to preserve an old system. They were the first prong that we plunged deep into the flank of our giant.

The colossal bulk of our institution cowered as we stepped back for another strike. Our second prong was sharp and true, and it cut a deep slash in the thigh of our opponent. Kingdom thinking redirected our focus away from central control. We started valuing individual gifting and destiny and went grassroots. Now the giant was hurting, weaker still. We pivoted and closed in again. With our third strike, we set apostolic initiatives free and empowered apostolic vision at a local level. Now all the prongs had connected, and our ultimate victory was only a matter of time.

The longer institutional toxicity persists, the more difficult it is to break free. Vision becomes limited. Disillusionment sets in. People lose motivation and eventually become numb, blind to the need to change. An oppressed mindset robs people of their 'fight'. They tried but the system pushed back, so they have no desire or drive to go there again. The more years someone has lived under the status quo, the more they have to lose if they challenge it. An institution can potentially destroy a person who resists. Someone can easily play the hero one minute and end up on the street the next, having lost any standing they had, along with all their relationships. Thankfully, the emerging generation owes the institution nothing, and they have little to lose. This means it is easier for a new generation to prevail, and in our movement, we couldn't have achieved what we did without them.

A CONSTANT TEMPTATION

Praise God, we freed ourselves from the institution that had constrained us over many years. It's amazing to stand on the other side of that ordeal and experience the relief. However, even with our 'giant' dead and gone—with apostolic initiatives thriving, the kingdom in play, and emerging generations engaged and leading within the movement—there is an ever-present tendency for us to slide back in the direction from which we have come. It sounds insane, but it seems to be human nature to voluntarily imprison ourselves. It's often there on the edge of the conversation, whining voices with an intent to derail healthy progress. They moan, criticise, complain, and sort of bite at the heels of everyone and everything that seeks to advance. Strangely enough, people quickly rally to the voice of the critical spirit. Maybe the lure is toward what is known, like a longing to return to slavery in Egypt.

Those who desire a return to institutionalisation are often motivated by their inadequacies. For instance, wouldn't it be useful to institutionalise the role of the apostle if I was struggling with my apostolic call? I could be an apostle in name only, without any need to embody the gift or demonstrate that I indeed carry an apostolic mantle. If I carry a whole lot of opinions that have never been worked out in practice, I might go to extreme lengths to silence my inner frustration and disappointment. I might even attempt to solidify my position at the expense of everyone and everything else.

Jesus' disciples asked, "Who's going to be in charge?" The more you are successful, the more that topic comes up. It has for us. Who will be in charge? Who will be the top dog? The questions are asked, even by good people with good hearts. Jesus chose good people but even they struggled with authority and power. In leadership, we gently navigate these dynamics with them. If we see people stepping into a trap of institutionalism, we will lead them around it if we can, and we encourage them in their walk with God.

People do not need quick wins or shortcuts when they are walking in heavenly intimacy and sensitivity to the Holy Spirit. In a life-giving environment marked by His presence and affirmation, people become strong in their faith and convinced of their identity and calling. Instead of relying on artificial structures, we can disciple them, encourage them and lead them into genuine kingdom accomplishment. Together with God, our desire is to help people live out their destiny *and* attain their heart's desires along the way, so that they are founded more deeply and endure for a lifetime, becoming champions of the freedom that makes communities flourish and enemies of institutionalism that does the opposite.

WAYWARD HEARTS

There's no accounting for our problematic hearts. We need others because the moment we separate ourselves, our hearts tend to stray. In an honest and Holy Spirit-filled community, God has the power to challenge us and ask questions of us, and good camaraderie can develop. When one of us turns to another and offers a tactless comment like, "Don't be an idiot," it can be a deep expression of love, care and concern. We have that now in Equippers. There's honesty and we're able to get real together. We balance one another, and our shared sense of kingdom purpose brings us together and continues to inoculate us against drifting away from our ideals. In the kingdom, there is abundance, not scarcity. There is enough for all. There's room for everyone to prosper in ministry and every other aspect of life. Potential relationships and alliances exist all around us because every one of us is on the inside of what is happening.

Independence needs to be avoided, not just because it can be a lonely path, but because a separatist perspective is likely to cause harm. People around us and coming up behind us can easily stumble and get out of sorts when they see leaders in competition with one another. If this mentality is not curbed, it will eventually grow into jealousy, causing a movement to regress until our relationships are so weak that conflict and offence develop. When there is a hollow feeling within individuals or groups, or they think that they are not enough and feel they need something to augment their position, they will often reach for institutionalism—or choose to withdraw. It is always better to reach out and freshly engage with community than to withdraw.

The same temptations come in times of success as well. When people think they've 'arrived' they often try to solidify that success, fearing the moment will evaporate and leave them empty-handed. When people are desperate it is easy to reach for answers in all the wrong places. A heart infected with comparison demands a competitive edge, and people who carry this competitive nature can easily plant the seeds of institutional thinking, attracting others who may feel similarly threatened. This puts the entire community at risk, and if the trend continues, these same people will soon have taken charge, and they will change the direction of travel for everyone. In these situations, institutions reemerge, kingdom culture recedes, the movement starts to stagnate, and people begin to look elsewhere.

How do we flourish? We must stay in faith. Faith holds to the vision we have been given by the Holy Spirit. It also defines our direction and informs many of the practical steps we will take to execute the vision. Faith binds everything together. We are laying hold of unseen realities, and by faith we need to express the vision in our conversations until it becomes tangible. If we disengage with vision or stop speaking about it as a community, faith starts to erode.

If we're struggling with faith, then hope also tends to wane. At that point, it's easy to drift or become lost. Our hope carries us between today's experience and the vision we hold so that it spans the distance. Without hope, we become vulnerable to lies and temptation until we are part of the problem rather than an embodiment of the solution we once were.

As a strong leader who is doing well, it is easy to step back from those who are not. But if we are living with an overflow of faith, hope and vision, we have an impartation to share with our brothers and sisters who are experiencing a 'dry season' or trying to find security by building structures rather than enjoying the freedom and organic nature of the kingdom of God. Thankfully, the kingdom has no taste for leaving someone behind. The apostle Paul noticed when someone was struggling, and he wrote:

> . . . *you who are spiritual restore such a one in a spirit of gentleness, considering yourself lest you also be tempted.*
>
> — *GALATIANS 6:1*

As a leader of leaders, you can generally tell the difference between those doing well and those who are not. It's natural and pragmatic to support what is working and resist what isn't, but kingdom culture prompts us to restore whoever we can. If a person was flourishing rather than languishing, they wouldn't need to reach for institutionalism. Christ values that seemingly difficult person over and above the movement. What is the deep work He wants to do in them—and in the relationship between the two of you? Is the real problem the fact that they are trying to fit a profile or become something they weren't made for? Is there a way to encourage them in a new direction? Is there a way to draw them back toward faith, community, and intimacy with Jesus? What would ignite vision within that person? When were they last flourishing as part of the community? How can you gently remind them of that? Some will need to be embraced to recover. Some will need straight talking. Others may even require professional counselling, but a generosity of heart toward the people we lead may become an antidote for the tendencies that threaten to undermine a kingdom community.

19

Kingdom Dynamics

We see the church as an environment where people flourish and grow in identity and maturity. From there, they confidently take their place in the world, bringing culture and expression into every sphere of life. Church leadership and kingdom living are designed to function hand in hand, but how do we establish environments where that is the case?

KINGDOM TRANSFORMATION

The church's responsibility is to continue to accomplish what Jesus began when He was here among us, and that is to manifest the kingdom of God on earth as it is in heaven. The church is an incredible force for good, but it can lose its way if it becomes self-indulgent and inward-focused. This is why we often say that we are to be "a church on mission" rather than "a church with a missions department". Reaching into the world is not an addition to the general operational life of the church. It is her core purpose! In the book of Acts, we see the early church proclaiming and demonstrating the kingdom of God, first in Jerusalem, then in Judea, and then to the outermost parts of the earth (Acts 1:8)! The church today needs to answer the question, "Where is our Jerusalem, where is our Judea, and where are our outermost parts of the earth?"

When Jesus came to earth, He brought the kingdom with Him. As He walked and talked and ministered, He was consistently declaring to all who would listen, "The kingdom of God has arrived" (Matthew 12:28, NLT). Then He demonstrated the reality of His proclamation through signs and wonders—restoring people's lives and livelihoods, renewing their health, setting people free, and bringing miraculous provision. The apostle summed it up on the day of Pentecost by saying that Jesus "went about doing good" (Acts 10:38).

The kingdom was—and still is, at heart—redemptive and restorative. Many people were repositioned through Jesus' ministry. A widow at a funeral for her son, who only saw poverty and desperation in her future, was completely transformed as she was given her son back from the dead. Another woman met Jesus by a well and socially moved from the fringe into the centre of her community. Jesus manifested the kind intentions of the Father's heart towards individuals, and the result was sheer joy, relief, and a pervasive sense that things were being restored to the way they should be.

Jesus was also *teaching* the kingdom. Our deepest motivations and attitudes are scrutinised through the lens of the kingdom. Are we ready, engaged, investing, and responsive to the challenge of extending His rule and reign? Are we the genuine article? In the Sermon on the Mount, Christ shared a vision of kingdom culture as a workable possibility for mankind. How do we reflect the culture of heaven in our attitudes and character? Turn the other cheek. How can we impact the lives of people around us? Go the extra mile. In other words, it is the state of our hearts and the way we think about others that matter most.

As the church, what are we valuing? The kingdom is within us, and transformation begins in the heart, but when we give heaven an entrance into our lives, it soon takes over the entirety of our being and overflows until it permeates the world we inhabit. As we enter our God-given place in the world, we become a conduit whereby the world can be filled from above. Nowhere is off limits, and any one of us can fill a role in society according to our calling, our gifting, and our assignment from heaven.

What does God want to do with our lives? How can we make this world a better place? How could He use us to transform the context we inhabit? Even the smallest seed can grow until the end product overshadows anything human plans or human reasoning alone could aspire to. The kingdom is invasive—like yeast in dough, unstoppable and impossible to control—and it takes hold as one person after the next catches on and takes their position within the master plan for the redemption of our world. One day, the restoration of all things will be complete, and all will be just the way that God intended. To embrace the kingdom is to set our eyes on that amazingly ambitious goal but humbly engage with a very finite and individual role, playing our part in what is a very tactile and temporal mission with a scope that is by no means confined within the walls of a church.

As we scan the words of Jesus and the apostles, we see that the kingdom demands a different approach from the world's way of doing things. We cannot build a life of significant kingdom contribution on the sand or with combustible materials. We need to build on something solid, and we are exhorted to build with things that endure (1 Corinthians 3:12). But how do we do that? How do we shape a legacy that is not subject to rot, rust or theft? We need to operate beyond the constraints of all that is passing away, fulfilling our mission and living in a way that will last. But what makes that possible?

EVERY CORNER OF THE WORLD

On the day Jesus ascended to heaven, He asked His disciples to wait for the Holy Spirit. If they had gone ahead regardless and attempted to build a heavenly vision in their own strength, they would have achieved little that was enduring, and at the very least would have formed only an institution. They would not have advanced the kingdom of God. There would have been no connection to heavenly resources, no uniting of lives with Christ in His glory, no ascension gifts or offices, no five-fold ministry, and no apostolic breakthrough. The early church would have had physical limitations with no supernatural power. If the disciples hadn't waited, they would not have been able to turn the world upside down as they did. They would not have been a transforming force or an answer to Christ's prayer that through them, the kingdom would come on earth as it is in heaven.

At the fall, the world was plunged into vulnerability and darkness.

Thousands of years later, through His sacrifice, Christ reconnected the physical and spiritual realms, reversing the fall and reinstating the potential for hope, goodness and light to permeate every corner of the world. He founded the kingdom on earth. Much darkness remains, even to this day. Holy Spirit environments allow the church to 'throw the switch' so that heaven's light fills the room, illuminating both the community and every person there through worship and wonder as well as engagement with the presence of God.

What about the rest of the planet? A pastor or a worship leader may be invited into a school or hospital to throw a switch and cast a little light, but the congregation's influence can be pervasive because the majority of those people belong on the inside. God's people are found all over the place. The incredible diversity of their vocations, associations, relationships and influence welcomes them into every sphere of life. They hold the keys to every kind of door that exists. When God's people go into environments where they already belong, they can throw the switch so that light penetrates the most ordinary and remarkable of places. The Holy Spirit graces them specifically to thrive wherever He has placed them. They are not just participants, they are practitioners who can demonstrate better approaches. They have ideas. They have talent. They are inspired, and they bring heaven's answer into their sphere of influence.

In the seventies, three apostolic leaders, each focused on equipping and mobilising the emerging generation, received a similar vision. Loren Cunningham, Bill Bright, and Francis Schaeffer were each given a blueprint that described how the kingdom of God could permeate the entire world. They saw the world divided into seven spheres of influence: business, government, media, the arts and entertainment, education, family, and religion. This was a 'master plan' for bringing about God's redemptive purposes on earth. It proposed that each believer who is filled with the Holy Spirit's power would receive an assignment in one of those domains. These believers would position themselves in that place and contend for breakthrough and blessing, transforming the culture in an organic way according to their natural gifting. This was a monumental shift. It challenged believers to fully engage in advancing the kingdom wherever God had placed them, and it created a shift in the church-centric mindset. The church was still essential for the edifying of the saints, but it also had a role in equipping and supporting the saints who were functioning elsewhere in outreach and ministry. Pastors and church leaders were positioned to bring kingdom transformation within the church, but the church was no longer seen as an end in and of itself.

SPIRITUAL POWER

When the Holy Spirit came upon the early church, the believers experienced the indwelling presence of Christ, and they were filled with power! They also received gifts, equipping them to be a wonderful answer to the needs of the world. God was outworking His plan for the complete redemption and restoration of mankind, and each had a part to play.

The ascension gifts belong to the church, but when leaders minister in their gifting, an impartation of heavenly power flows, and it cannot be contained. When a highly gifted and mature leader is upfront, it is not so much about what they are doing in the moment as what they are *awakening* in the lives of the congregation. The spiritual power associated with each of the five-fold gifts naturally reproduces life and empowers those who may never occupy a formal role or title inside the church.

An anointed leader, walking in his ascension gift, establishes a school to equip an emerging generation of prophets, evangelists, apostles, pastors and teachers—and now heaven can touch down in any environment. An entrepreneur breaks through with apostolic authority to disrupt an industry. A project manager navigates baffling complexities with prophetic insight, bringing downloads of wisdom from heaven. Others might bring a pastoral heart into a hospital ward or a lunchroom. The essential ministry gifts operate in their purest form within the church setting, but they empower and influence leadership far beyond the bounds of the church!

There is also a spiritual power available that is tailored to each individual believer which we call their motivation gifting (Romans 12). There is a supernatural edge that each of us brings as a contribution to the kingdom.

This is true for any environment we are in, whether 'secular' or 'sacred'. For the prophet, this is supernatural insight; for the servant, supernatural energy; for the teacher, supernatural wisdom; for the exhorter, supernatural favour; for the giver, supernatural resources; for the ruler, supernatural authority; and for those with the gift of mercy, supernatural empathy. Our motivational gifting enables us to operate effectively within our distinct sphere of kingdom influence—and beyond!

OUR DUAL PURPOSE

The church is described as the body of Christ—one body with many parts—demonstrating to the world an incredible truth: "Christ in us, the hope of glory" (Colossians 1:24-27). As believers, our desire is for God's glory to fill the earth. His desire is that each of us is changed "from glory to glory". The message of redemption is being outworked globally and locally, collectively and individually.

Kingdom perspectives have matured over the last thirty or forty years, and with it, our understanding of the mandate Jesus gave us. The great commission calls us to not only share the Gospel and baptise people into relationship with Jesus but to disciple and teach them as well. The good news is a message of salvation—and restoration!

But there is another aspect to the duality of our call, and it reaches beyond the individual. The conversation includes a focus on discipling communities and nations by exemplifying and introducing wisdom, righteousness and kingdom culture into secular environments.

When we come to Christ, we become agents of change. We are ambassadors of heaven! In other words, wherever we go, everyone—regardless of their relationship with Jesus—can experience a touch of heaven in their natural environment. They may not know why our ideas are so good, why our work seems so inspired, why we understand what people want and need so intimately, why we love and care so well, where our capacity comes from, or how the breakthrough arrived—but they know the real thing when they see it, and heaven's manifestation is irresistible.

When we carry the Holy Spirit into a room, those around us come alive. Ideas flow. Differences are settled. Details that may have been overlooked are noticed. As agents of Christ, we are bringing tangibility to His words: "The kingdom of heaven is near." We are carrying the kingdom right to where people are and intertwining it so closely with their lives so that they can observe and enjoy—even unwittingly—the dynamics of the kingdom among them.

When we carry the mind and spirit of Christ into an organisation, a family, or a community, we are welcoming the kingdom into that place. We are showing people what happens when Christ rules and reigns in our lives. We want to bring individuals to Christ, and we share the gospel whenever we can. But in every interaction, we can bring a taste of heaven on earth in a way that is deeply meaningful and personal to them. We are setting people up for an encounter with Jesus by solving their problems, sharing our insights, and showing them how we do things in a way that blesses and benefits them. We are acknowledging that our mission is twofold: to see people restored in their relationship with their heavenly Father, and to bring kingdom transformation to every corner of the earth.

20

Quality Leadership

As a movement, we are called to be an apostolic company of people benefiting from different graces, and a diversity of giftings. People are initially impacted within a church context, then they ripple out to become a living manifestation of the kingdom in whatever place God has called them to. This context and mission shape our leadership.

THE TWO SIDES OF LEADERSHIP

When we look at the ascension gifts, we find diversity and commonalities. ACTS Churches have been on a journey to express the five-fold ministries primarily as a way of equipping and undergirding people so they can become everything Christ has called them to be. Apostles bring victory. They break new ground and create a space that others can occupy. Prophets enable people to see their role and destiny. They bring hope, vision and direction. Evangelists uphold the priority of the Gospel, ensuring the good news of Jesus remains a central focus, and leading people to Christ. Pastors cultivate safe and nourishing environments where people can receive the word of God for themselves. They position people for growth and soul restoration so they can be strengthened in every area of life. Teachers help people gain understanding and provide language for what we often already know intuitively. Their insights bring depth and richness to our work and life.

For us, apostolic leadership is depicted by an 'under-rower' or servant. We support and value people so they can give their best—and *be* their best. We enable their work to succeed. People do not exist to serve our vision, we exist to support them! We shifted away from a solo leadership model to valuing complementary leadership teams made up of a diverse range of gifts with a focus on grassroots enablement. We have reinterpreted five-fold leadership by applying kingdom thinking. This has led to an *inter-connected model* in preference to a *centralised model* of leadership.

Scripture refers to leaders as elders, pastors or bishops. These leadership titles are often interpreted as three distinct leadership roles or positions; however, my understanding is that these are the three responsibilities of every leader: we oversee people as a bishop, shepherd them as a pastor, and eventually, bring experience as an elder. Paul brings these three aspects of leadership together in his letter to the church in Ephesus. Speaking to the *elders,* he writes:

> *Take heed to yourselves and to all the flock, among which the Holy Spirit has made you **overseers**, to **shepherd** the church of God which He purchased with His own blood.*
>
> — *ACTS 20:28*

Peter does the same in his first letter:

> *The elders who are among you I exhort, I who am a **fellow elder** and a witness of the sufferings of Christ, and also a partaker of the glory that will be revealed: **Shepherd** the flock of God which is among you, serving as **overseers**, not by compulsion but willingly, not for dishonest gain but eagerly; nor as being lords over those entrusted to you, but being examples to the flock; and when the Chief Shepherd appears, you will receive the crown of glory that does not fade away.*
>
> — *1 PETER 5:1-4*

The point is, although there is diversity among the leadership gifts, there are common traits and ideals as well. We are all called to *come under* people with our support, but we are also called to govern and to *provide covering* for their safety. When people struggle or fail, we ensure they are protected and valued while they work through issues. At the same time, we provide vision and resource-rich environments so that others can flourish.

PRESSURE AS A POSITIVE

As leaders, pressure eventually works to our advantage. The challenges we face shape us by provoking a reaction in us that can build our faith, develop our character, and supply the grace we need to keep moving forward. God showed the apostle Paul that the unrelenting pressure he dealt with brought him into a greater dependence on God, which in turn gave him the strength to continue, despite the pressure (2 Corinthians 12:7-10). The difficulty Paul faced became an opportunity for God's grace to manifest in his life and ministry.

In this world, pressure is usually a signal of danger—and if we see it this way, it can lead us to respond in fear and distract us from our calling. But if we refuse to be diverted, remain humble and keep a grace-infused kingdom perspective, the pressure has no ability to derail us. Instead, God's grace will surround us and safeguard us despite the vulnerability and weakness we may feel. Pressure builds our resilience, and we begin to feel the pressure becoming tolerable. This is evidence that greater leadership depth has been formed within us and that God has used the pressure not only to empower us but to extend our gifting!

In his first letter, the apostle Peter called pressures by a different name. To him, they were part of the 'trials and tribulations' we all face, not something to be considered a strange or troubling event (1 Peter 4:12). Pressure is to be expected if we are engaged in leadership within the kingdom, and it varies in nature for each individual. Some face problems with their health, others struggle financially. I faced opposition and jealousy over any progress we had achieved. Whatever it is, pressure is guaranteed to come to us all, and if it causes us to call out to God, He will respond with grace, and we will be enlarged.

HANDLING CONFLICT

One of the responsibilities of leadership is the need to train others and ourselves to navigate disagreement. To do this, we need conviction and an open mind, thick skin and a tender heart. If we entertain rejection because our opinion isn't heard, it won't be long until we have removed ourselves from the game, and whatever vision, anointing or gifting we carried will become fruitless. Differences of opinion are a natural part of life, and we need to grow in our ability to handle this if we are to fulfil our calling. Our ability to argue well and objectively is an important skill because our point of view is as valuable as anyone else's and deserves to be represented in the conversation. But we also need to listen—and open our minds to those who may disagree or come at things differently to us.

I praise God for a father who invited good debate and engaged with me on difficult topics. I've done the same with my children, encouraging them to express their opinions and lift up their voices. Working through things thoroughly is important in our families and marriages, in our work and ministry, and in our friendships. Navigating differences is an essential leadership and life skill, and bringing confidence to the process helps both us and the people we live or work with.

When we carry apostolic vision, we need to bring other leaders along with us, while drawing out and respecting what is in them. Often this happens in meetings, and as a leader, when you're in a room full of strong-minded people, you need to manage the dynamics of the conversation. I like to set parameters around how things will work in this environment—for example, we can argue about issues, but we will not touch character. The moment we label someone a 'liar' for example, we have gone too far. Often, we need to be patient and slow things down in order for others to be heard—or to grapple with the issues. We also need the tenacity to build consensus. Most importantly, we need to be gracious, honouring people, crediting their intentions, and pursuing mutual respect and trust with everyone. When we continue to engage with those who may disagree with us, without letting other's words or their treatment of us define us, God's grace can fill our meetings and pervade all of our relationships.

I have found that the most difficult conflict situations do not arise because of well-intentioned people. They arise because of an opposing spirit. In these instances, it is essential to discern between the person in front of you and the spirit that may be in the background. Perhaps there is jealousy or fear. In any case, the devil loves to find a seat in the room. We know our wrestle is not with people (Ephesians 6:12), so it is essential that we learn to oppose the spirits of darkness while valuing the person who might unknowingly be under their influence. Jesus could pull off saying to Peter, "Get behind me, Satan!" but in most cases, this would not end well for us.

We can't move the kingdom forward unless we deal with disagreement properly while exemplifying its culture and ideals. If I suspect something is lurking behind a person's perspective, I do not confront it directly. Instead, I ask questions. "What do you mean by that?" "Where does that come from?" If someone responds, "Everyone's saying . . ." I would reply, "Well, who's saying . . . ?" In doing this, we are providing a challenge. We are testing the spirits. We're patiently taking it back to the person until there is a sifting in the conversation. We're exercising grace and understanding while we sort through what has been said. In other words, we disregard the pressure of the situation and the temptation to take shortcuts that could ultimately dishonour another knowing it is worth the process to give whatever is hidden time to reveal itself.

Normally, it all comes out in the wash when we do this, whereas direct confrontation only polarises the room and results in issues remaining unresolved. Our discernment grows as we lean toward resolution and unity for the sake of the whole. Throughout it all, our posture remains the same—we are looking for good, robust conversations that pursue the truth in a manner that honours people, their thoughts, and the Lord, whose heart is for us all.

TEAM FORMATION

To be effective, a visionary leader needs to surround themselves with a team of leaders who can help implement what he or she sees. Not everybody is a visionary. Some are wired to serve and flourish in a vision-filled context, and good leadership enables that. Well-functioning teams are made up of a great blend of people with diverse gifts. I think the ideal size for a visionary team is seven, but five is a good number to start with. Anything smaller than that can lead to a loss in traction, and with more than seven there is a risk that the quiet team member will become quieter, and the noisier ones will talk more. It's worth avoiding that dynamic because everybody's contribution is valuable.

Whatever the size of the team, there is a need to share the vision, invest in others, and draw out the diversity of their gifts that will help bring the vision to life. To cover the distance, fulfil the God-given mission and maintain longevity, we need a range of gifts. A leader may be capable of administration, but if it's not their core strength, it would be wise to find and empower others who have that particular gift and skill set.

Once we have formed the team and gained some momentum, other things are required to keep everyone travelling together. A regular check-in is essential. When I was the national leader, we held meetings regularly, and every meeting had an agenda so that everyone knew what would be covered. I asked someone to take minutes so we all came away with a record of what was happening and what was decided. I tried not to schedule team meetings at night. Instead, we would go to a restaurant and enjoy a meal together following a day's interaction. We wanted to relax and relate with each other as well as do business together.

It's important not to dominate. As the leader, you need to set the direction of travel, but you need to remain open. People respond positively to strategic direction, and it's good when they contribute their tactical ideas and perspectives, but when the consensus moves in another direction, it's important to be patient. You need to know and care for the people in front of you. Your team may not be quite hearing what you're saying, or you've got it wrong, or the timing is off. In my mind, you don't want that to happen too often. Good leaders need to get direction right ninety percent of the time. Anything short of that will quickly erode the team's confidence. The main thing is that you draw out the participation of the whole team, because as the leader you need to hear from everyone and value all the voices in the room.

21

Apostolic Leadership

The story of Paul and Barnabas is a great example of how a community can support apostles who are still in formation. The early church leaders heard from God and their prophets affirmed what He was calling them to do. Then they said, "Come on, let's release them." Paul and Barnabas were recognised and set apart, but the early church did not instruct them about what they should do. Instead, they prayed and fasted together and encouraged them as they set out on their journey. Paul and Barnabas went into regions where there was no distinct kingdom expression and established communities of believers along the way. Apostolic obedience was a defining characteristic in both of their lives, and even when a sharp division arose between them over John Mark, their travelling companion, and Paul and Barnabas went their separate ways, both men stayed true to what God had called them to do. But it was the leaders of the church in Antioch who ultimately enabled the vision because they recognised and released Paul and Barnabas rather than restricting them.

CRITERIA FOR SUCCESS

When apostles are able to quickly follow through and engage with their God-given vision, we call this 'apostolic immediacy'. It is a term I picked up from an older man. He was a prophet, and he challenged us to create an atmosphere, like in the early church, where apostles were free to express what God had placed on their hearts. The leaders in Antioch created an environment where Paul and Barnabas could function in apostolic immediacy, and there was great kingdom benefit as a result. These men would push into new territory and the ground they won for God would be hard fought, but other leaders were behind them, supporting their endeavours.

This dynamic is essential. Paul and Barnabas could have remained in Antioch, where there was significant work to do, but instead of being held back, they were enabled. Pressure in a role forges apostles for a time, but they also need room to explore their gift with some degree of release and freedom. Apostles need to hear from God and act quickly, without undue hindrances from others. They are meant to take ground in fresh ways, engage with new opportunities, and execute vision with a sense of haste.

Apostles generally operate at the periphery of a movement or an apostolic house, and for this reason, they need resources that they can apply in their field of operation. It can be soul-destroying for an apostle to raise funds that could be used to extend their vision, only to have them diverted into maintaining the organisation and leaving them short of what they need for their work. That's the sort of system we were up against in our early days, and it was frustrating for me and others who were similarly minded.

As our movement continues to grow, we know that one central hub is not able to service the entire scope of our vision. This is why we have apostolic houses. They are 'hubs within a hub', enabling resources to stay closer to where they are needed. We want resources to serve the vision. There is a timing component to apostolic immediacy, meaning we need to ensure resources are available as the vision develops. If we keep operations as close as possible to the action, we can better support apostolic initiatives. There's a saying: "Opportunity is often missed because it's dressed in overalls and looks like work." Apostles aren't daunted by hard work. They see something that looks like a big job, and because they have a passionate response to a challenge, they're innately prepared to put the required effort in. They're energised by it!

Apostles have a God-given internal drive, and if we create a healthy environment around them, they will naturally thrive. But attitude and personal formation are also important in the life of an apostle if they are to step properly into their role. There is a cost to be paid along with the call, and the apostle needs to make a choice. It takes faith to step into something when you do not yet have all the answers or the personnel or the resources you need. An apostle needs to be prepared to go 'out there' with the absolute confidence that God is going to provide for them, and to persevere with obedience and energy until they see the tangible manifestation of what they envisioned in the beginning. The apostle will grow alongside the vision, and a vision will always attract resources. As leaders of apostles, we need to surround them and support them as much as we can, because if the apostles are doing what they are made for, everyone can ride on the back of what they achieve.

THE MAKING OF AN APOSTOLIC LEADER

One of the apostles who came after me says that one of the best things I did for him was to stand back and give him time and space to fail until he eventually became an apostle in nature as well as in calling. Apostolic leadership is all about the apostle's development. It's about growth and maturing. It's about letting people go through a process so that God can shape them the way that He wants and build in them the message and mandate that He desires for them to carry. That takes time—and patience.

Someone once remarked that apostles don't come to any place of significance or maturity until they've been on the journey for about twenty years. It only takes about half that time for a pastor to develop, because as soon as a pastor is deeply rooted enough to live in overflow, they can exercise their gift to an ever-increasing degree. It is much the same for a teacher. Once they have developed a robust wisdom framework for their own lives, they can share that with others and gently grow in influence. Apostles, however, need to develop a kind of 'critical mass' of God-given identity, authority, and vision—enough to break through for real usefulness and impact. Then they cycle through that process again and again, and every win makes them stronger and more effective.

The apostle John was a young man when Jesus called him, yet his gospel, his letters, and the book of Revelation were written well towards the end of his long life. Consider the weightiness of his words, and what they convey in terms of his authority and experience of God. As an old man, he could see further and more clearly, and he articulated the vision in a remarkably enduring way. He is a wonderful example of an apostle who kept growing in authority and effectiveness within the kingdom.

We will certainly experience ebbs and flows as we move to new levels in our leadership—we may even feel for a time that we have gone back to base one. However, in each successive season we have more to offer, despite the pressure we experience or the mistakes we may make along the way. The Church needs apostolic fathers who create an environment where younger apostolic leaders can grow and mature through trial and error. Each of us has learnt something through our failures that can be of benefit to others. Pain, pressure and struggle are important for the formation of an apostle. These things challenge our hearts. It's so easy in life to get offended, and difficulty will certainly come, but there is one issue that differentiates between an apostle who will endure and grow in effectiveness, and one who won't last the distance: How we deal with offences.

Paul and Barnabas faced offence and overcame it. Ultimately, they reunited, moving past the disagreement so that they were able to fulfil what God had given them to do. Conversely, Judas Iscariot became bitter and harboured offence, and this ultimately opened a door for the devil to overtake him. As apostles, we need tough skin but a soft heart, and often the struggles we face during our formative years are designed to give us just that. If we are soft-skinned, vulnerable to jealousy and rejection, and susceptible to insecurity, then when tensions arise—as they inevitably do in leadership—we will become hard of heart.

We must learn to weather the environment without losing our gentleness of spirit, in order to last the distance. We must forgive readily and release people from our judgment, and we must deal with our fears and insecurities.

All of this is part of the formation of an apostolic leader. They become less vulnerable, more mature, more confident—and more patient! They are able to work with other apostolic leaders without being threatened by them. It is a sign that a person is progressing as an apostle when they can see the success of others and be overjoyed by it.

THE APOSTLE IN COMMUNITY

God packs so much into a single individual when He creates an apostle, but they need to understand that they are not able to function alone. They need to live and work within a community. An apostle's view of others can make or break their effectiveness and determine the longevity of their influence. If they have a hierarchical view, they will see themselves as the boss and everybody else is seen as a means to fulfil their vision. Instead, they need to value the different grace gifts that God has placed around them and be able to work alongside them all. When an apostle works with an anointed teacher, the teacher can bring understanding and language to apostolic intuition. They can often articulate the vision more deeply or relay it in terms of a richer biblical context. When we were thinking about apostolic communities, Steve Graham, who is a great reader and researcher, was able to quickly pull together a historical overview for us. A prophet can respond to apostolic vision by bringing direction to what God is saying. I remember a prophet coming up to me once and saying, "You think you've been called to London to build a big church, but God has called you to be an apostolic father over here [Europe]." What we now have in Europe came out of that prophecy. When the entire community with all those gifts is functioning well, it is so powerful. Acknowledging gifts ignites gifts, and the apostle is well-placed to lead in that. Our gifts are enhanced by working together and acknowledging the grace gifts that other people carry.

APOSTOLIC BREAKTHROUGH

Some ministry gifts are meant to maintain what has already been established. This is important because we can build on something if it has been well cared for. But it is a mistake to think of this as an apostolic work. Apostles bring the breakthrough. They take ground. We send them to a new place, and they usher the kingdom of God into that area. This is not to say they own the cutting edge of the kingdom or that no one else can inhabit the space. Others can facilitate breakthrough by bringing a strong prophetic voice, but we need to change the thinking that apostles can be stationary and manage churches. While a prophet can facilitate kingdom breakthrough, they will tend to do that by themselves, whereas the apostle can mobilise the whole community to that end.

In the New Testament, the apostles came into an area and created an environment where the church was established and then started to flourish. Every Christian is personally able to partner with God for breakthrough in their time and place, but an apostle will leave a legacy that continues. A strong pastor, for example, may shepherd a growing church, but often the church will decline in numbers when that pastor is no longer in leadership. That shouldn't be the case if we have good apostolic leaders. If the same pastor worked alongside an apostle, their influence would be as great, but what they accomplish could last longer. In the same way, an apostle will weave a prophet's influence more deeply into their community enabling them to leave a legacy that is larger than any specific prophetic word.

WHAT IS AN APOSTLE?

The word 'apostle' didn't start with Christ or even with Christians. The word was originally used in the Roman Empire and was *adopted* by the early church. This realisation helped me reframe my thinking about what modern-day apostles in the church should look like. In Roman times, the word 'apostle' was used of someone who was officially *sent*—either as a commander of a shipping fleet or special envoy over land—to extend the reach and the influence of the Roman Empire. The Romans thought of apostles as those who served the Empire by ensuring the culture and ways of Rome were established in new regions and nations around the world. In other words, apostles were not just 'sent ones'—they were sent *with a purpose.* The early church applied the name 'apostle' to those God had set apart for kingdom expansion.

This rings true with what Christ's first apostles actually did. They were not focused on one location. Instead, they travelled far, blazing a trail and enlarging the influence of Christ's kingdom. Thomas went to India, Philip to North Africa, Matthew to Ethiopia, Bartholomew to Armenia, and Simon went as far as Persia. These early apostles fulfilled the true meaning of the word as they found ways to express what Jesus had spoken over them in John 17. Aware of the huge responsibility they carried, Jesus prayed powerfully over them, asking the Father to sustain and encourage them as they gave themselves to fulfilling what God had given them to do. "I've been with them, but now it's up to you, Father," He was saying.

Seeing apostles as those who fundamentally reach far and wide has challenged my thinking and prompted questions in my mind. So many apostles today are staying at home and governing, rather than going out and travelling and being true to their calling. The calling of apostles is to be 'ambassadors for Christ' (2 Corinthians 5:20). They represent another sphere, another kingdom, but their responsibility is not just to represent it. They are there to *implement* it. They are planting churches, they are redrawing the borders, they are creating structures and environments where people can say 'yes' to Christ and His kingdom. They are tasked with bringing kingdom expression and enabling communities to adopt kingdom culture.

When apostles are released, faith, hope and vision can flourish. Their lives seed positive change all around them, because when the kingdom finds expression in people, it can touch down in nations and communities as well.

22

Personal Formation

God is intimately involved in all that we do—but He is also deeply invested in *who we become.* As we engage with the specific mandate and purpose He has for each one of us, God's desire is that we would all be changed so that we reflect His likeness (2 Corinthians 3:18). He is taking us from glory to glory by the Spirit of the Lord!

In Paul's letter to the Philippians, he writes:

> *Not that I have already attained, or am already perfected; but I press on, that I may lay hold of that for which Christ Jesus has also laid hold of me. Brethren, I do not count myself to have apprehended; but one thing I do, forgetting those things which are behind and reaching forward to those things which are ahead, I press toward the goal for the prize of the upward call of God in Christ Jesus.*
>
> — Philippians 3:12-14

Paul understood the individual calling on his life, and he determined to lay hold of it with as much fervour as God had shown in laying hold of him! In the kingdom, what we are given to do and who we ultimately become are intimately linked.

EMBRACE YOUR MANDATE

We each have a unique identity and purpose, and our leadership contribution builds on that critical foundation. We are to lead according to His master plan for our lives, and we will each give an account of how we have stewarded our God-given gifts and responsibilities—whether in the church or in the secular realm.

We may have a particular gift profile and understand our purpose well, but this doesn't always mean that we have the role to outwork it. What can we do when we are not in a position to fully execute the vision God has given us, or exercise the potential we carry? This is a common question in local churches. Many people think they need the position of a pastor to be one, but the truth is, there are many ways to pastor people! Small groups can be a wonderful setting for outworking a pastoral gift. The same principle is true of all the ascension gifts. Whether you are an apostolic leader or a prophet, an evangelist or a teacher, there is always something to do in the interim. While the frustration of waiting for a 'position' to open up is often inevitable, we must be careful to not develop a divisive or rebellious spirit. If we are tempted to linger there, we will eventually find ourselves far away and even 'out of bounds' in terms of God's will for us! When we have a position, we naturally have more freedom to express our gifting, but in the meantime, we still carry leadership and vision within, and it is important to find a place for this to function.

For many years I carried the vision for our movement but was not in a position to outwork it. During that time I was always provoking and asking permission to bring change. Sometimes that worked, sometimes it didn't. In the meantime, however, I led the Auckland church well and embraced the global reach that God had placed within me. Eventually, the opportunity developed for me to step into the role I needed to fulfil the vision.

If the vision is from God, God will always go before you. He will develop opportunities that you can take advantage of. His timing is very important. The last thing you want is to be hamstrung in your role because things haven't fallen into place quite as you envisioned. You can be in a leadership position and still be restricted from fulfilling your destiny. Patience is required as we hold out for God's best. It is not easy to be in this place of tension, however, because vision is energising and often has a feeling of urgency attached. As apostles, we must act on vision with some degree of haste, but wisdom and timing are important also. A healthy relationship with authority and the structure around us is vital. The same faith-filled hope that releases vision, strengthens our conviction and stirs us to take action, also has the power to sustain us as we wait.

One of the reasons timing is so important is that we can't execute our vision alone. We can't make a significant kingdom contribution as a solo agent. We want to take people on a journey with us rather than trying to simply implement things by ourselves, and the honour and respect we need from others is gained over time.

Helen and I nurtured people and led teams well before I was given the position of national leader. I had asked for permission to shape things, but there came a time when I miraculously received it, and only then could I reach further. Some people say, "Give me the position and then I'll do the job." My response is, "No, you start functioning, and then the position will come." Our criteria today is that people are functioning before they have the position. Many of our emerging leaders passed this test and now have great influence and endless scope to function.

UNDERSTAND AUTHORITY

David had the anointing to be king well before he assumed the position. In the meantime, he demonstrated submission to both God and those who were in authority. This is a great testament to his character. David knew that he would one day inhabit Saul's position, but he refused to behave in a way that would undermine the role that would eventually be his. He was true to himself, but he didn't overreach. He bided his time, and slowly God gave him people who would help in the outworking of the mission. He didn't need the position of a ruler to get started as one! He attracted the destitute, those in debt, and those on the margins, and he formed them into an army. Before David had any formal position, he worked on the fringe and found ways to benefit the kingdom he would one day be given.

A position carries authority, but your gifting carries an intrinsic authority too. A position may give you more scope to operate, but you can take ground wherever you find yourself, simply because you have a gifting! Luke 16:1-12 teaches us that God rewards those who are faithful with what they are entrusted with. This is true when it comes to the stewardship of finances and of things that belong to others. Sometimes our role is to serve another, and when we do this well, it doesn't escape God's attention. Whatever we steward will be rewarded with more responsibility and scope. If God wants us somewhere, He's going to put us there eventually. If we're faithful, He will make it happen!

LASTING THE DISTANCE

Leadership takes passion and resilience, and it comes with many challenges. Significant contribution carries a cost—but if we are unable to last the distance as a leader, we risk it all coming to nothing. Without longevity, how can we have a lasting impact for good?

For me, longevity as a leader is about getting the basics right. Without any sense of legalism, Helen and I are both very good at having a consistent devotional life. It's simply part of who we are. We are personal worshippers before we are public worshippers. The Word of God is an important part of our devotional time, and we also journal. We've been consistent about this all our Christian life, and the power of this cannot be underestimated. Longevity in ministry comes when everything flows from our personal relationship with Christ. Maintaining our alignment with Him requires constant attention, but it's worth the effort.

When people are trying to respond to Christ's call on their life, they often go 'all out'—and in doing so, they 'lose out' on a few important things. Eventually, if we are not careful, we can sacrifice our marriages, our family, our health—and our longevity in ministry! God wants to look after us as people, and He wants us to look after ourselves as well. I don't see my responsibilities as a list of priorities. I can't afford to play one thing off at the expense of another. My life is not hierarchical like that. Instead, I see my life more like a wheel with lots of spokes, and Jesus in the centre. God smiles upon me when I'm out in my boat fishing because He knows that I'm replenishing myself. God smiles upon Helen and I when we go out for a meal together and focus on one another. God smiles upon me when I'm in a business meeting and I'm working. God smiles upon me when I'm having a family night with my grandkids. I received the analogy of life as a wheel early in my Christian life and it has given me a sense of balance ever since.

It is important to be present in all our relationships, but especially those at home. As a significant leader, there will always be demands on your time and attention, and if you are married and have a family, you need to discuss how you are going to make that work together. I determined that I was going to be present for my children. I never saw my role as a father in opposition to my call as a leader and a pastor. The same is true in our marriage. In recent years, I have done a lot of travelling, and Helen has had a great level of involvement with children's ministry. Helen and I needed to work out what that would look like. We needed to discuss how we would handle our times of personal separation, so we could find a sustainable approach in marriage. We are both on the same track in terms of faith and ministry, but because we have different calls and giftings, we're not always going to be doing everything together.

For me, recharging is key. At night, as much as possible, I like to shut down and take a rest mentally from the responsibility I carry. The need to fulfil vision is significant, but there's only so much that one person can carry, and I know myself well. I know my personality, and I know that to be able to operate at a certain level of leadership and vision, I need time by myself. It's a priority. If I take time to recharge, I can be fully present and have something to give when I am with people.

One way I survive a busy life is by going home and giving myself space. I still need that when I am travelling, so in those times, my hotel room becomes my home. I choose not to stay with other people because I need space to refill my reserves. I've learnt that I can work incredibly hard as long as I do that. Not all of us are wired that way. I've got friends who are replenished by being with people. We are all different. The main thing is that we understand ourselves and what we need to do to stay at our best. We need to stay in peace. Our strategy for longevity may be amusing to others, but that doesn't matter. I've earned the nickname of 'Bolter' because I move into an environment strongly and with conviction, do the things I need to do full of energy and passion—and then I 'bolt', I'm gone! In other words, I step in and contribute, and then step back to recharge. Perhaps more than anything, this is what has allowed me to have a sustainable life and ministry.

CULTIVATING A PROSPEROUS SOUL

Having a prosperous soul is important because it affects every aspect of our lives. Ultimately, if we're not thinking well of ourselves, this will impact our body, our life, our marriage, and our relationships. A prosperous soul is not about wealth or money, it is about feeling good about ourselves and being comfortable in our own skin. First and foremost, soul prosperity rests on the foundation of our relationship with the Lord.

I love David's expression of a deep and healthy relationship with the Lord. In Psalm twenty-three, he's walking with the Good Shepherd and receiving care in every aspect of his life. Every statement David makes throughout this psalm is a faith statement that all of us can relate to on our journey.

The Lord is my shepherd; I shall not want. (v. 1)

God cares for His people. With every new season that unfolds, there is a relevant answer to our need for provision. God will meet our needs—whether it be a house, a job, finances, health, or whatever it takes to fulfil our calling.

He makes me lie down in green pastures; he leads me beside the still waters. He restores my soul. (v. 2,3)

God is committed to ensuring that we are refreshed and replenished. He is intentionally leading me, restoring me, rejuvenating my soul, and making me a healthier, better person. Sometimes that involves dealing with some pretty serious matters. For a while, I leaned toward being impatient and slightly short-fused. When Helen challenged me about this, I had to come before God so He could help me deal with my responses and give me a more restful soul—a *restored* soul.

He leads me in the paths of righteousness for His name's sake. (v. 3)

Having a prosperous soul comes when we're open to the Shepherd's desires for us. He leads us in paths of righteousness, making sure you and I always walk with integrity. I don't have a hidden cupboard anywhere, and when I travel by myself, I don't come home with any form of guilt.

Yea, though I walk through the valley of the shadow of death, I will fear no evil; for You are with me; Your rod and Your staff, they comfort me. (v. 4)

God is changing how we think about ourselves. The more our perception aligns with His, the less inclined we are to lower ourselves and revel in things that could potentially degrade or derail us. We may walk through some pretty dark valleys at times, but we don't need to fear when faced with threat and loss, because our Shepherd is with us.

You prepare a table before me in the presence of my enemies; You anoint my head with oil; my cup runs over. (v. 5)

Life can throw some unexpected curve balls, especially in the area of our health. A prosperous soul leads to an ever-increasing propensity toward general wellbeing. It is possible, however, to be dealing with very real physical problems or health issues and still have a prosperous soul. God tends to us through these times, filling our cup to overflowing. When our soul prospers, we have abundant reserves to draw on, even in times of pain or difficulty.

Surely goodness and mercy will follow me all the days of my life;
and I will dwell in the house of the Lord forever. (v. 6)

God gives us promises to sustain us throughout our leadership journey. But we also carry some responsibility for the wellbeing of our souls. Like David, the people we keep company with affect our ability to stay the course. I want to be surrounded by those, who like myself, have chosen to seek and possess a prosperous soul. It is easy to let the wrong people speak into our lives, but I have learnt to not listen to every opinion. Not everyone has our best interests at heart, or the interests of the kingdom. David determined that he would not dwell in tents of wickedness or keep company with those who were not flourishing. Instead, he chose to dwell in the house of the Lord. He kept company with those who shared his heart for God.

STRENGTH OF HEART AND MIND

Scripture reminds us that those who wait on the Lord will receive strength. That strength may look different for each one of us—in any given scenario we may need strength of conviction, strength to accomplish a task, or strength of mind to lead in wisdom.

Strength of mind is essential. We must recognise thoughts that could have a negative effect on our health and wellbeing, and bring them into captivity. The most effective way to keep our thinking in alignment with God's is to meditate on His word. God's word sustains us, makes our lives fruitful, and allows us to prosper in all we do. I want that for myself, and I want that for us all.

It is important to remember that a person can be strongly anointed, carry great leadership authority and influence, and be very charismatic, yet their soul may not be prospering. We must all be careful about this. Benny Hinn once said, "I gave so much time to the anointing of my ministry, I forgot who I was as a person. It affected my marriage, and I lost everything." If we are to last the distance in every area of life, we must continually care for the state of our soul.

A prosperous soul leads to an ever-increasing propensity toward general wellbeing. But there is one factor in leadership that is critical to our longevity, and it is our strength of character. There is a big difference between our gifts and our character, and ultimately, deficiencies in character will disqualify the use of our gifts. In many ways, we can measure the prosperity or fruitfulness of our lives in terms of outcomes, but the prosperity of our soul is measured by personal wellbeing, our sense of identity, and most of all our character. When you get that right, positive outcomes generally follow, and not the other way around.

A FATHERLY WORD

As I reflect on my own personal formation and think of those who have set out on a lifetime of ministry, the greatest encouragement I can bring is this:

Read and keep reading. Study and keep studying. Meditate and keep journaling. Pray, and learn to pray with authority. Don't just ask, learn to command and receive. Have confidence in what you've heard from God, and walk in it. Embrace the power of desire as the precursor to God speaking. The desires of the heart are very important. A redeemed desire is as powerful as the voice of God speaking from heaven.

Walk out your convictions. Don't be surprised if things don't work out immediately. Everything has its time and season. Make sure that you're constantly attentive to the prophetic sound around you. Learn to listen, not only for yourself but for other people, because the prophetic shapes destinies.

Don't be afraid to move quickly. Not all decisions need time. When the vision in you demands immediacy, act quickly so you don't miss the season. If Jesus knocks on your heart in the middle of the night, respond to Him, because that moment may not be there in the morning. Know how and when you hear God best. Enjoy the Holy Spirit and revel in His presence.

Every time you stand to act, keep humility of heart and the right attitude. Always trust the Holy Spirit to use you. Don't take for granted the prophetic unctions that God gives you. Learn to trust and value them in the moment. Look for the sound of something precious in others, and trust the intuitive voice of God more than your reason, because it is more reliable. Push for more. You can operate at a higher capacity. Don't allow feelings of weakness to rob you of God's destiny, because ultimately your destiny will become your strength.

23

Fathering

My father was a great dad, but he died when I was relatively young. Over my years in ministry, few people have been able to step into that role for me but there was one who did, Pastor Marcus Goulton. He was an older man who invested in me whenever there was an opportunity. Pastor Marcus carried a spirit of faith for the miraculous as well as for missional endeavours, and this had an invaluable impact on my life.

Paul understood the need for spiritual fathers. In 1 Corinthians 4:15, he writes:

> *For though you might have ten thousand instructors in Christ, yet you do not have many fathers; for in Christ Jesus I have begotten you through the gospel.*

Paul observed a dynamic in the early church that concerned him. Plenty of people were clamouring to lead, but there was a distinct lack of fathers. The same is often true today. One person wants to be everyone's guide, another wants to bring understanding or tell others how to live or seek to organise everyone! But those who are willing to be fathers are a rare and valuable breed.

Paul came to the place in his life where he saw the power and the importance of fathering. A few years after establishing the church in Corinth, he recognised that they had run into a lot of difficulties. The church was in crisis—they had division, problems with their sexuality, and issues stemming from dabbling with the occult. Paul could have come in with a heavy hand or the attitude of a superintendent. He could have come in as a teacher, unpacking the truths they needed to understand, but instead, he wrote to them as a father.

His posture as a father was what the church in Corinth needed. They were not in the kind of headspace where just any leader could speak into their situation. They needed someone who could come in gently but firmly, someone who could say, "I'm not here as your mentor or your teacher. I'm here to be a father to gently but firmly restore and recover those who have lost their way. I'm here for your betterment."

THE HEART OF A FATHER

Fathers understand that it is pointless to come into difficult situations with a heavy hand. What is needed are those with a father's heart, and this is not confined to gender. Helen is a good example of a woman who carries the heart of a 'father'. She has spoken at women's conferences all around the world and could be enjoying the fruits of what she has sown in ministry over all these years. Instead, she saw the potential in the children of our Auckland church and became the children's pastor. People know that she may have far more influence if she were travelling the world preaching, and they ask her, "What are you doing this for?" The reality is, she can see the value of legacy. She is expressing a father's heart for the next generation.

Fathering does not come from a position of power or a need to control a situation. It comes from a desire for people to flourish. This world is a difficult place in which to lead and operate in the ministries and calling to which God has appointed us. Leaders need fathers who will undergird them, encourage them, and impart loving wisdom in the face of crisis, chaos, or despair.

Perhaps the prophet Malachi foresaw a day when the hearts of the fathers had grown cold or become distracted by other things. He saw how easily a fatherless generation can fall to curses and dire consequences. When we downgrade the role of fathering we develop an orphan society. When fathers are absent, the blame for society's problems and sometimes willful choices—along with the responsibility to fix them—is often laid at the feet of the emerging generation. But in the book of Malachi, we read of a day when:

> *. . . he will turn the hearts of the fathers to the children, and the hearts of the children to their fathers.*
>
> — *MALACHI 4:6*

It's the heart of the fathers that must turn first, not the other way around! When fathers begin taking responsibility for an orphaned society and stepping up to take their place, not as leaders but as fathers, our homes, churches and communities will flourish and be restored!

THE POSTURE OF A FATHER

In Luke 15, Jesus tells a parable that gives us insight into the Father-heart of God. In this story, we see a son who has been degraded. He was born into a loving home, surrounded by all he needed, but with one foolish decision, his life took an unexpected turn. Still, he stubbornly clung to his rebellious and entitled mindset, until finally he hit rock bottom, and with no dignity left, he began the long walk home. Amazingly, none of that mattered when the father caught sight of his son and ran to embrace him!

As Christian leaders, we must embody the same attitude as the father in Luke 15. Notice he did not chase his son down the road or seek to prevent him from his course of action. He let him go his own way, knowing the deep formation that would come by allowing him space to repent of his own mistakes.

On the face of it, the father's reluctance to intervene doesn't look like love, but over the years I have come to understand that it takes a deeper sort of love to see a person go through situations that could potentially destroy them and to hold onto faith and hope for that person even when the individual has none for themselves. It takes the heart of a father to not give in to fear.

This scripture has provoked me for so many years. Am I a father who constrains the outcome or acts with force on behalf of those I love? Or do I give people freedom to fail, and wait without judgement for them to repent? Am I willing to use all my energy to create an environment of lavish welcome rather than to cajole someone who just isn't ready? When people repent, how will I treat them?

I have learnt that it's okay for people to fail, and it's okay to stumble. We cannot protect our leaders or even our children from all the blunders that they will make. I think a father knows that. We think the world of them and know they are bursting with potential, but we understand that their formation is a process, and they will experience bumps along the way. As fathers, we are not owners, we're stewards. We are here to steward people into their destiny in God.

LEADERS AS FATHERS

Often in our churches, too much has been built around a charismatic pastor rather than on developing a culture of genuine care for people. This has created heroes of many leaders, rather than fathers.

For much of David's life, he had been the hero. He had taken out giants, won mighty battles, and united the nation under God. Now, all that had changed. David knew he would not be the one to build the temple or to lead Israel into the days ahead. His time had come to step aside. But instead of seeing himself as 'sidelined', David became a 'sideline supporter'! With his own work now done, he turns his focus to supporting his son Solomon in the glorious assignment he had been given by God. It is a pivotal transition in David's life, but there's humility in his response. He understood that he was no longer the leader of the nation, but that he was—in every sense of the word—called to be a father.

When the time came for me to hand over Equippers to Sam, my son, something fundamental shifted. My ability to father rather than simply lead the movement increased. This dynamic plays out whenever a leader chooses to stand aside and allow the emerging generation to come through. It forms something in us because it involves another level of dying to self. Handing over the leadership of ACTS Churches New Zealand and Equippers was a great decision for the church, and from that point on, it was less about me. But it also formed something in me because in stepping down, I needed to learn to trust God and to trust Sam, who was relatively young at the time. Thankfully, we knew it was the right move.

BECOMING A FATHER

It seems as if God has been working away on us for years, and then we discover that while we thought he was shaping us into great leaders, what He had in mind all along was to shape us into a father, just like Him. When we realise this has happened, we have a choice. Will we resist the moulding and the shaping and yearn for our days of leadership, or will we embrace the incredible privilege of being a father?

Fathering is a choice. When we serve, we tend to operate out of our gifting. But when we become a father, we operate first and foremost, from our heart. We long more than anything else to see others prosper, and this changes the nature of our service. A pastor will teach and establish, but a father will go to greater lengths to gain someone's heart and hold their attention. They are motivated by love more than by care or responsibility, but that love creates a deep desire for vigilance and protection.

Interestingly, it does not take an old or even middle-aged person to be a father. A younger person can often embody the heart of a father. It's about how we treat people and how we relate to them.

For me, it took a lot of preparation to have the heart of a father because by nature I'm an incredibly bossy person. I like to control my environment and without God's redemption, I could easily have become cruel. Thankfully, in my early years of leadership, God spoke to me about this. I tended to see others as beneath me, until God said, "I want to change the way you look at people. I want you to come under them. I want you to serve them, not control them."

This adjustment to my heart involved a relentless process of dying to old habits and beliefs. It began when we first arrived in Auckland. Everything in our life had been preparing us for that moment. Being called to pastor the Auckland City Church presented a significant opportunity as well as a great responsibility, and it could have gone to my head. But God began speaking. "This is about the future," He said. "Many churches have risen to prominence only to disappear just as quickly."

When I heard that, something in me decided, "We're not going to be that church." Until then, we had always asked God to show us what spirit we were dealing with in the location we were in, and how we should counteract it. In this case, it was the spirit of prominence. Auckland was seen as the city where 'the big dogs won'. To overthrow this spirit, we needed to counter-weight with humility. This required some fine-tuning of my heart. My whole attitude needed to change.

Today I am so grateful for God's work in me and on me during that season of my life . . . and into the next! When my children were approaching their teenage years, He once again challenged my tendency towards control. While as parents we set firm boundaries around our children while they were young, I now had to learn to loosen my grip and allow them more space to make their own decisions. This led me to ask all sorts of new questions about my children and my role in their lives. What is our relationship becoming? How will I love them now? How will I be a father to them in their adult years? It was my fatherhood journey that flowed over into the way I led in the church. I was grappling for the right balance. I was asking questions of God. It was new territory, and over time, I learnt to trust more. My confidence as a leader was reshaped until it was rooted in a foundation of love, not fear, and it changed the trajectory of our entire life and ministry.

THE NATURE OF FATHERING

In the book of 1 John, we find an interesting distinction between fathers and those who are less mature. Although the order is unusual, the message is clear. John writes:

*I write to you, little children, because your sins are forgiven you for His name's sake. I write to you, fathers, because **you have known Him** who is from the beginning. I write to you, young men, because you have overcome the wicked one.*

— 1 JOHN 2:12-14

Children need to be loved and shown grace, and young people need to win their spiritual battles, but the thing about fathers is simply that they know their God. They have experienced life, and their relationship with God has stood the test of time. When you meet a father and sit down with them, you come away thinking, "That's a man (or a woman) who knows God." Their knowledge of God is the gift they bring to those around them.

I never set out in ministry with the role of a father in mind, but in recent times, as I have found myself taking on this role in our ACTS and Equippers movements, I have begun valuing it more and more. I can sit down with a pastor today and ask very direct questions, not from an attitude of intimidation or condemnation, but knowing I can help in ways I never could have as a younger person. But we need to be careful as fathers not to create dependence. When the statement is reversed and we talk about 'spiritual sons or daughters', we must not imply that they will always be our 'sons' or 'daughters', or that these younger people are under our authority or control. We must always be mindful that the success of our ability to father is measured in our ability to bring others to a place of maturity. If a person does not have the freedom or ability to live their own lives, make their own mistakes, and find their destiny without our help, we've let them down.

There's no reward for creating dependence. We labour to present everyone complete in Christ. That's the father's mandate. This doesn't mean that we can't be acknowledged as fathers. I used to feel uncomfortable whenever people referred to me as their spiritual father, but these days, I value it. They are simply saying they find security in me, and when I see the world they must navigate day by day and understand the power of what a father can bring, I am simply convinced we need more and more leaders who are committed to making this transition.

LIKE OUR FATHER

Jesus brought a manifestation of the kingdom wherever He went and in every interaction while He was here on earth. But the most powerful aspect of Jesus' life was seen in His relationship with His Father in heaven. "I and my father are one," He said. "As my father taught me, I speak." "I see the father working, and I work" (John 10:30, 8:28, 5:19).

While the role of a father is precious and pivotal, it is our relationship with the Father in heaven that is to be guarded and treasured above all else. Jesus enjoyed deep communion with His Father, and He carried the Father's heart as He went about establishing the kingdom and doing good.

God's heart is to "bring many sons to glory" (Hebrews 2:10), and as fathers, we join Him in that desire. We look beyond the stumbling, the bad days, the struggles and self-doubt, and as we come alongside with kindness, patience and fatherly determination, we join Him in raising one after another up, affirming them in all God has called them to do, and reminding them of who they truly are—sons and daughters who bear His likeness and have been graced and gifted to minister powerfully in His name.

As fathers in the faith, we are becoming to others what He is to us. When we position ourselves to understand the heart of God the Father, something of the cloud of His glory comes to fill our humanity. We experience restoration and fullness in His presence, and we extend the fatherhood of God into the world. It comes down to being fathered by God ourselves. We experience His heart and allow it to overflow into the lives of those we serve and love. In my mind, this is the ultimate expression of leadership.

I now travel around the world in a representative role. What I find, is that people want someone to talk to. They want honesty. They don't want someone to take over or tell them what to do. I've achieved what I was given to do, but other people are in the midst of living out their calling, and I can lend my story and experience to them. I can listen. I can pray. I can support and even just be there as they grapple with vision and identity. My season at the frontline is done! I can genuinely say that I live for the success of others rather than myself.

In Philippians chapter three, the apostle Paul writes, "I have suffered the loss of all things, and count them as rubbish, that I may gain Christ and be found in Him" (v. 8, 9). Paul had served as an apostle; he had run his course and finished the race. Now he was reaching for one thing only—to be found in Christ. He was laying hold of something that was not about accomplishment. He had moved into a fathering season, and as his identity adapted, so did his ministry.

I'm beginning to understand what that is like. I want to pass from this life to the next with my boots on, but I have no desire to be working at the same pace I did in the past. In one stage of life and ministry we had to cover everything. But in this season things are different. I can still preach, but I can also sit beside a young man and help him through a crisis, or walk with people in marriage difficulties. On any given day I may be speaking to people who are spinning out from life's pressures—or to those who are thriving and surging with leadership potential! It is a sweet and satisfying place to break into. As fathers we become the embodiment of what it means to be blessed to be a blessing.

And so, I bless you. If you are called to be a father, may you be transformed into His likeness by the Holy Spirit and carry His heart for others. If you are a leader, I bless you in your life and ministry, your family and your marriage. If you are young in the faith, I lay claim to your potential to grow until all that's left is Him shining in and through you. The Lord bless you and keep you. The Lord make His face shine upon you and be gracious to you. The Lord lift up His countenance upon you and give you peace (Numbers 6:22-26).

The ACTS Partnership Manual and Local Church Trust
Deed template are available to view online at:

www.monkministries.com/trust-documents

www.ingramcontent.com/pod-product-compliance
Lightning Source LLC
Chambersburg PA
CBHW021631120626
46545CB00002B/493